THE MEDICINE OF THE PEOPLE

D1491653

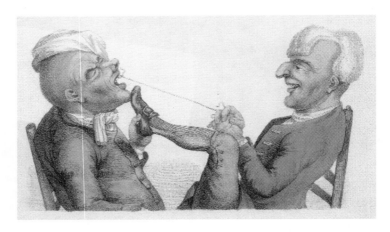

'Laughter and Experiment', depicting a common form of amateur dentistry. Tim Bobbin, *The Passions Humorously Delineated* (London, 1810). (John Rylands Library, Manchester.)

THE MEDICINE OF THE PEOPLE

A history of popular medicine
before the National Health Service

Allan Chapman, M.A., D.Phil., F.R.A.S.
Wadham College, Oxford
Faculty of Modern History, University of Oxford

 AENEAS PRESS, CHICHESTER

Published in 2001 by
Aeneas Press
PO Box 200
Chichester
West Sussex PO18 0YX
England

Copyright © 2001 Allan Chapman

All rights reserved

No part of this book may be reprinted, reproduced or utilised in any form
or by any electronic, mechanical or other means, now known or later
invented, including photocopying and recording, or in any information
storage or retrieval system, without the prior written permission of the publisher

British Library Cataloguing-in-Publication Data
A catalogue record of this book is available from the British Library

ISBN 1-902115-04-X
Printed and bound by MPG Books Ltd, Bodmin, Cornwall

꙼ APR 15
0051372
610. 9 CHA
1 week loan

To the memory of my maternal grandparents,
Albert and Lily Platt, of Pendlebury, Lancashire,
whose curious lore first aroused my interest in the
Medicine of the People

Contents

Illustrations

Acknowledgements

I wish to express my gratitude to all the people who supplied me with material for this book. Many of them are no longer alive, for the process of accumulation has been slow; and in the case of many others, I have no knowledge of their whereabouts. My verbal sources have come down to me via many routes, and only over the last twenty years or so have I committed them to formal notes immediately after the telling. Like many of my respondents, I picked up the Medicine of the People, as they did, by casual conversation. In addition to the suppliers of this early stock – sometimes gleaned in passing conversations with persons whose names I never knew – I wish to thank those who wrote to me and who permitted me to interview them formally.

I also thank my friends in the medical profession, mainly in the Liverpool and Manchester areas, for their own recollections of folk medicine as encountered in consulting room explanations of what their patients believed ailed them. Unless I have been able to obtain my respondents' permission to publish their names, I follow the practice of citing vernacular sources under the person's initials. Like all vernacular traditions, the Medicine of the People is rooted in gossip and a love of story-telling, and I wish to thank those people, including elderly members of my own family, who not only told me their tales, but who also inspired in me a desire to pass them on.

I also wish to thank Robert Marriott for his work on the design, graphics, editing and indexing of this book.

My largest single debt of gratitude should, however, go to my wife Rachel, for typing, reading and proof-reading so much of the text, and for offering her suggestions and insights.

The author and Publishers are also grateful to the John Rylands Library, University of Manchester for permission to use 'Laughter and Experiment': Tim Bobbin, *The Passions Humorously Delineated*, on the cover and frontispiece illustrations.

'The Organ in the Court': a typical congested slum of the mid-nineteenth century – in this case in London, although it could easily have been in Liverpool or Leeds. Gustave Doré and Blanchard Jerrald, *London: a Pilgrimage* (London, 1872), p.176. (Author's collection.)

1

The people's health

Western European and American people living in the latter part of the twentieth century belong to a unique generation in the history of mankind. From the time of Julius Caesar to the early years of Queen Victoria's reign, the overall life expectancy remained little changed, as a range of incurable fevers and other diseases killed off most people before they reached the age of forty. The rich, being better fed and living in more comfortable circumstances, might reasonably expect a marginally longer life than the poor, but the vast majority still died very young by present-day standards. A modern person living on unemployment benefit is likely to live longer and enjoy better health and more physical comfort than a medieval king, and would have considerably better odds in favour of surviving a serious illness than would a Victorian millionaire. It was only after World War II that the majority could reasonably expect to reach the Biblical span of three score years and ten, and this came as the culmination of a revolution in medicine and public health which extended, in practical terms, to little before 1840.[1]

Not only do modern people live in much better physical circumstances than those endured even by their grandparents; they also have wholly different medical expectations. For centuries, medicine was a conservative art, operating within close limitations which were seen to be as eternal as original sin. Sickness had, after all, an important moral dimension which, for Christians and Jews, was one of the consequences of the Fall of Man, while even pagan classical Greeks had been willing to ascribe it to the Fates. If sickness was, therefore, a corollary of human pride and a divine affliction, there was little hope in trying to substantially overcome it. God in his mercy, however, had given man a limited knowledge of how his sufferings could be mitigated, and this constituted the art of the physician. While one might expect certain physicians to be older or wiser in the practice of their

1

art than others, none were considered capable of bringing about radical progress. What was seen as applying to one generation or nation was seen as applying to all, in the same way as the Plague of the Philistines also attacked the Children of Israel.[2] Roughly speaking, the illnesses and curative procedures which had prevailed in the Greece of Alexander the Great were the same as those to be met with in the French Court of Versailles under the Sun King. Though the doctors of the medieval Arab world, such as Avicenna and Alhazen, had made significant innovations in particular aspects of medicine such as the anatomy of the eye, these innovations were related more to medicine as an intellectual discipline than as a curative art.[3] They represented research as yet incapable of development.

It is in our concept and expectation of medical progress that we constitute a unique generation. The great majority of modern people see medicine as a reliable technology which has, over the course of the last century, wiped out one major affliction after another, until only a relatively small number remain to kill us. Few now view medicine as operating within a general moral and religious context, although this belief was resurrected by those who promulgated a divine cause for AIDS. We now expect to live longer lives, free from pain and even mental distress, and we are caught dangerously off-guard and unprepared when we find that this is not possible. One hundred and fifty years of public health, a century of pills, injections and operations, and fifty years of psychiatry and socialised medicine have given us a wholly new set of expectations.

Our generation is also unique insofar as it is better informed and educated than any before it. In spite of our concerns with teenage illiteracy and school standards, there is more real knowledge penetrating deeper into all levels of the population than ever before. The man in the street will learn considerably more about the countries, resources and circumstances of the world from television news and documentaries than the most intelligent child would have done in an Edwardian Board School. A young mother of average ability, if she attends her pre- and post-natal clinics, will pick up more about the reproductive process than the most intelligent and inquiring Victorian woman, for whom accurate information on this subject would have been virtually unobtainable. A knowledge of germs and bacteria, no matter how imperfect in its technical aspects, provides ordinary people with a framework in which to practise intelligent domestic and personal hygiene. Such basic information, one must stress, is no longer the prerogative of certain social groups made privy to it by education or social standing, but has become the general culture of the many. It can be held on all levels of sophistication, from systematic education at one end to a form of implanted folk-instinct at the other. In the sections of the population whose medical knowledge has not been systematically imparted – those who are not trained doctors and nurses – it is hardly surprising that many of the features of an earlier and sometimes archaic medical culture survive, often cheek by jowl with a familiarity with the modern usage of antibiotics, heart transplants and psychotherapy. It is the form in which these medical archaisms have survived, and still permeate our thinking on medical matters, which is the subject of this book.

Before attempting to trace the origins and persistence of the earlier medical culture, and the way in which it has survived into the very recent past (and even into the present), it is important to say something of the overall medical environment still prevailing at the end of the nineteenth century, to place it in context. If high mortality and general suffering were regarded as part of the human lot, it was because of certain limitations which the environment placed on early modern medicine, against which the physician possessed no resources. These limitations related to the hygienic, dietary and social habits of the people.

Well into the nineteenth century, the most prevalent and the most deadly class of disease was fever, in its various forms. Until the development of the bacterial theory of disease in the second half of the nineteenth century, the source and origin of most fevers was held to be the same as in ancient Greece. Fevers were thought to come from 'miasmas' or 'contagions': clouds of unwholesome air which

3

somehow poisoned the bodies of those who breathed them. This concept of epidemic disease, which had been discussed at length by Hippocrates four centuries before Christ, and had been used to explain the outbreaks of bubonic plague in the Middle Ages, was still held responsible for the first waves of cholera that struck England in 1832.[4] Though the medical profession was aware of the distinction between diseases like cholera, which seemed to be 'in the air', and specific person-to-person infections like syphilis, it had no adequate explanation, let alone cure.

Smallpox had been the first of the great killers to be successfully curbed, when Dr Edward Jenner realised that a person developed an immunity to smallpox (which was the most lethal killer disease of the 1790s, when he was doing his research) if he or she had suffered a prior infection of the much less dangerous cowpox. Though Jenner knew nothing about bacteria, or how this immunological principle worked in scientific terms, his vaccination technique was to save countless lives, and by the twentieth century led to the virtual obliteration of smallpox.[5] Cheap and simple as vaccination (from the Latin word for cow, *vacca*) was, however, smallpox still continued to ravage the population throughout the nineteenth century. It is astonishing to realise that a disease which could be wholly prevented (but not cured once caught) in 1800 should still have been claiming victims in major European cities a century later, and it says much about the general ignorance in which many Victorians must have lived concerning medical matters. Victorian literature is often a mine of information about health and medical attitudes. In Charles Dickens' *Bleak House* (1854), the heroine almost dies from preventable smallpox which nonetheless still ruins her beauty, while the same disease, described with full clinical horror, claims the life of Zola's courtesan, *Nana* (1880).[6] The terror with which Nana's friends flee from her, once she is infected, makes one wonder how widespread was the practice of preventive vaccination, at least among the Parisian *demi-monde*.

Epidemic diseases in one form or another continued to claim the majority of lives until well into the twentieth century. By the late Victorian period, bronchitis and tuberculosis were the major adult killers, and in 1901 accounted for some 550 registered deaths in Salford.[7] It is true that death rates had fallen considerably between 1840 and 1900, but this was due more to a triumph in public health and the better administration of towns than to specific medical discoveries on a scientific level. Such figures as Edwin Chadwick and Southwood Smith, whose efforts had led to the founding of the Board of Health in 1848 and the passing of the first Public Health Act in the same year, had made the people's health a matter of Parliamentary and civic responsibility.[8] Sanitation was improved, while Dr John Snow's demonstration that cholera was transmitted via contaminated drinking water rather than through aerial 'miasmas' constituted one of the classic pieces of medical detective work.[9] Liverpool, in the late 1840s, was a more dangerous city in which to live, from a medical point of view, than most medieval towns had been. Its first Medical Officer of Health, Dr William Henry Duncan (who was also the first publicly appointed M.O.H. in the country), provided statistics for 1848–50 from which we deduce that in each generation born, more than 70% would be dead before reaching their mid-forties. In the first ten years of his appointment as M.O.H., Dr Duncan recorded in his 1857 Report, the death rate had averaged 36 per 1,000, although this included the great cholera epidemic of 1848.[10]

Half a century later, in the 1901 Report of Dr Tattersall, the Salford Medical Officer, it appears that less than 3% of the City's 221,526 population were over sixty-five.[11] Manchester, Liverpool and Salford were the nation's blackspots from a medical point of view, where chronic poverty, ignorance and despair raised seemingly insuperable obstacles. In 1901, when Salford still had a death rate of 21.7 in 1,000, more prosperous and less congested towns like Oxford had only 13.85.[12]

An absence of effective personal hygiene must also have played a part, while this absence itself derived from a number of factors. Before the development of a more easily available plumbing technology in the late nineteenth century, bathing was beset with many obstacles. The production of adequate quantities of hot water was both expensive and tiresome, even for the rich. Poor personal hygiene, however, was not seen as a major social obstacle until well into the nineteenth century; even then it was still considered somewhat effeminate for a gentleman to bathe too frequently. Such old British heroes as Dr Samuel Johnson had been legendarily proud of their personal effluvias, while the late Georgian socialite, Topham Beauclerk, boasted that he carried enough lice upon him to 'stock a parish'.[13] Samuel Pepys, an otherwise fastidious gentleman of the late seventeenth century, frequently found himself to be lousy, and in January 1669 'cleansed' himself of some twenty lice.[14] Among the poor, with their over-crowded houses and lack of fuel, one can only assume that adequate washing was rarer still, hence increasing their susceptibility to typhus, the classic 'fever' which we now know was transmitted by person-to-person vermin. This was responsible for many of the 'low' or 'burning' fevers which often exhausted and emaciated their victims. As the nineteenth century progressed, however, regular bathing came to be seen as a genteel prerequisite, and one of the ways in which the poor came to be characterised was as 'the great unwashed'.

Some Victorians came to begin the day with a bath – usually a cold one. The Reverend Francis Kilvert, for instance, sometimes delighted to note in his Diary how the ice on his bath water had first to be broken. Charles Dickens became attached to beginning the day with a shower bath that was so powerful that it was called the 'Demon'. However, we must not forget that to many Victorians a daily douse in cold water was seen as washing the soul as well as the body.[15] Whether many members of the Victorian working class went in for similar rituals before going early to work on a winter's morning is not recorded. D.H. Lawrence mentions the frequent coal-dust-removing scrubs of Edwardian colliers, though these went no lower than the waist.[16] On the whole, however, much nineteenth century hygiene was concerned with the dirt that showed, and if a man always kept his body covered, he could hardly get it dirty! It needed the germ theory to radically alter this deeply entrenched opinion, and this did not make a major mark on the medically untutored slum-dweller until after World War I.

Considering the damp climate and the poorly constructed houses in which the Victorian working classes lived, keeping warm and dry involved a whole set of logistics in its own right. The loving mother's concern for the wet feet of her household provides an excellent case in point. I remember asking a Pendlebury lady why, if wet feet caused colds and pneumonia, were sailors not constantly dying from these diseases? I was confidently told that while rain water is a source of mischief, sea water is not.

Such popular aphorisms as 'Ne'er cast a clout till May is out' also tell us much about hygiene, warmth and damp, encapsulating traditions passing back through the Victorians to the pre-industrial world we have lost. The prescription of woollen or flannel garments next to the skin did not only mean that such a fabric should be worn through the winter months, but that the same piece of fabric must remain in place for that duration. As with the hair shirts of the medieval ascetics, I have encountered several examples of elderly persons who spoke of people – usually children – wearing the same garment all through the winter earlier in the twentieth century. Weak chests, in particular, derived much benefit from being encased in the same flannel liberty bodice from October to May. Such procedures, no doubt, drew strength from the Englishman's obsession with chills and draughts, whose pernicious influences were always hovering ready to enter any pores which had been foolishly opened by winter bathing or momentarily stripped of their flannel armour.[17] The language of the Medicine of the People is frequently reminiscent of a battle of wits between the healer on the one hand and the semi-demonic predator of disease on the other. No matter how houseproud a Victorian working-class housewife may have been, or how well-scrubbed the hands, faces and collars of her family, the unregarded invisible dirt and bacteria which surrounded them must have been a major factor in the high mortality rates endured.

In addition to the problems of private and public hygiene, three other factors exerted deleterious effects upon the population, especially the poor: bad diet, alcohol and opiate preparations. Now that the Victorian and Edwardian periods have receded far enough to be invested with a romantic aura, many people have come to believe that food was fresher and more nourishing and that ale was 'real' at the turn of the century. This has, moreover, been an image successfully cashed in upon by the purveyors of certain wholefoods and 'natural' products. There is, for instance, a northern chain of bakeries, Allinson's, who marketed a brand of bread which was said to have had 'nowt taken out', and was skilfully promoted by a plain-speaking north-country Victorian character.[18] Another brand of bread, Hovis, was, well into the 1990s, being promoted in television commercials to the sound of brass band music and nostalgic scenes of life in Edwardian Pennine villages. Bread is, one may suggest, a convenient foodstuff for this style of selling, because its bran content harks back to the Victorian obsession with bowel movements. The Baxenden piemakers Holland and Company quite recently advertised their confessedly excellent products as possessing a 'taste of the good old days'.[19]

Some years ago I read on the label of a popular brand of breakfast cereal the statement that as modern foods are so chemically treated it is necessary to add bran and other 'natural' products to prevent constipation. The advertisement went on to state that in our great-grandparents' time foods had been natural and untreated, in consequence of which constipation had been virtually unknown. I think that it would be hard to find a more distorted use of medical folk beliefs and a more blatant contravention of the Trades Description Act, and I was not surprised to see the advertisement withdrawn from circulation. What this tells us, however, is how easy it is to distort the past and fabricate a concept of the health of our ancestors in the promotion of commercial products. In reality, the Victorian working class was almost congenitally constipated – a fact witnessed by the age's obsession with brimstone and treacle, castor oil, and patent medicine purges. In the words of the unnamed sage of Greenock: 'Fear God, and keep your bowels open.'[20]

Victorian foodstuffs were often appallingly adulterated, especially when intended for sale to those sections of the population least likely to resort to litigation. Milk was skimmed and mixed with starch to make it appear thicker. Bread, which was often made from industrially refined cheap white flour, was further whitened with alum (especially in the mid-nineteenth century), and given bulk with cheap ingredients such as potato-, bean- or pea-flour. Tea was adulterated with miscellaneous leaves and earths to add to its weight, not to mention dried second-hand tea leaves. Far from being the romanticised 'real ale' of today, Victorian beer was often watered down, laced with salt, brewed from cheap industrial sugars and mixed with iron sulphate to bring a good head on a poor brew.[21] The use of poor-quality chemicals could lead to dangerous adulterants such as arsenic getting into the brew, and between 1898 and 1901 one hundred and seven heavy drinkers were found by the Medical Officer of Health to have died in Salford from the presence of this chemical. Butter was adulterated with gelatine and even rag pulp, while sugared confectionery could be tinted yellow with chrome salts, blue with Prussian blue, and green with copper arsenite. The passing of the Adulteration Acts of 1860 and 1872 began to restrict the most blatant abuses, but not until the mid-1870s did the public analysts begin to make a serious impact.[22]

Even assuming that unadulterated supplies were available, Victorian food preferences were often very unhealthy. Amongst other things, the Victorians were confirmed lovers of red meat and fatty animal products such as suet and dripping, which they consumed in proportion to income. No one who looks at the recipes in Mrs Isabella Beeton's *Book of Household Management* (1861) or the works of her imitators can doubt the extremely carnivorous character of the Victorian upper classes. Vegetables, when eaten at all, tended to be over-boiled, and thereby reduced in nutrition content. Meals were often large, and one can understand why both men and women wore corsets, and a 'chubby' look was fashionable.

Working-class cooking, rather like lifestyles in general, frequently came as close to that of their 'betters' as finances would allow. Butcher's shops serving the poorer districts inevitably sold the poorer cuts of meat, and, as refrigeration was not available on a general scale until the Edwardian period, products were not always fresh. One needs little imagination to realise the state of the meat being sold under such conditions in the hot days of summer, and why diarrhoea and similar disorders were regarded as common summer ailments. For those too poor to patronise even the slum butchers during the normal day's trading, it was often possible to buy 'scrag ends' at the end of the day, and especially on Saturday evening, when the week's unsold scraps were sold off to feed dogs and paupers.[23] The working-class housewife was not so much a cook as a culinary miracle-worker. If the family were poor – that is, surviving on under £1 per week in 1900 – finding a sufficient quantity of food was often a problem. For this reason, she became skilled in the employment of water and cheap vegetables to spread the flavour of the meat through the greatest possible edible bulk. This was the secret of the Lancashire hot pot. Such a dish was often very filling, as far as bulk was concerned, though bland to the palate. Herbs would then be used to spice it up, and plenty of salt to give it 'bite'. Robert Roberts, in *The Classic Slum* (1971), also mentions the great popularity of fried foods in Edwardian Salford – a popularity emphasised many times by elderly people who provided information for the present study, and by the general condemnation of such food by visiting doctors.[24] Frying, after all, was a fast and simple way of preparing a savoury meal from the cheapest ingredients, and is still one of the most popular working-class culinary techniques. Fried dishes were (and still are) widely eaten accompanied with large quantities of bread, covered in the past with dripping, but now with margarine. The popular cafeterias on the promenades of Blackpool, Southport and similar seaside towns still boasted, during the summer of 1987, 'Fish, chips, peas, tea and bread, £1.30'.

The more affluent working class would also express their superiority to the 'common sort' in their food preferences. The wives of artisans would insist on 'best butter' for their tables, and speak with contempt of the 'waggon fat' magarine which graced the sandwiches of the unskilled and improvident. It is interesting to note how fried foods have retained their popularity, and how – with the exception of the American hamburger and the Italian pizza – fish, chips, pies and 'butties' have remained conservative favourites since the industrial revolution.[25]

When considering these dietary conditions, one finds an almost tailor-made formula for health problems: poor-quality meat of dubious freshness, insufficient protein, far too much carbohydrate and a confirmed preference for white bread. Too few vegetables and most of them over-boiled, too much salt and pounds of animal fat all contributed to the short lives of their confirmed eaters. Yet when one contemplates the above diet, one can forgive the old working class for that sweet tooth gained in childhood and never lost. Refined sugar was one of life's few joys, and one ate as much as one could get, in sweets and domestic preparations. Eggs could also provide an invaluable dietary supplement, and many colliers reared hens (and illegal fighting-cocks) in their back yards. It says much about the overall scarcity of eggs, however, that a whole egg was generally reserved for dad, who would give its top by way of a treat to the chosen child.[26]

Most cooked food was prepared on open ranges above coal fires, which must themselves have added their own unique pollutants to an already inadequate diet. The alarmingly low health standards found among the volunteers for the Boer War in 1900 caused Parliamentary questions to be asked about the British Bulldog's capacity to fight a major European war.[27] As well as leading to Lloyd George's reforms after 1906, they drew attention to the poor state of working-class cooking and nourishment. By the early 1900s, Board Schools in many districts of northern England were providing cookery classes for girl pupils, as well as instruction in how to make and wash clothes. Well-intended as these innovations may have been, their practical results do not seem to have been as significant as expected.[28] The respondents to Elizabeth Roberts' survey on this subject seem to have shown that little of value was eventually taught, while my own mother, who received such instruction in the mid - 1920s, said attention was usually devoted to fancy cakes rather than basic food making. Another major drawback to these school cookery classes was the fact that the ingredients had to be paid for by the girls themselves, and few mothers had the spare shillings to finance their daughters' efforts in burning teachers' decorative inventions. Most girls, it seems, continued to learn whatever cookery skills they acquired at home, and these could be precious few.[29] It is probably true to say that most working people had already learned how to obtain as much nourishment as possible out of the resources available, and any real improvement had to come from a higher standard of income and living, which was a factor that did not significantly alter until after 1914.

One very common condition of the period resulting from the poor dietary and living conditions was rickets, or bow-leggedness, which could run through entire families. Though now known to be the result of a vitamin D deficiency, it was popularly ascribed to its sufferers having been 'put on their feet too soon' as babies. Adults who manifested this conspicuous deformity were said to be unable to 'stop a pig in a ginnel'.

To the survival diets of most working-class families in 1900, alcohol added a further problem, in addition to claiming some 40,000 lives per year.[30] Not only were precious shillings from the family budget wasted upon it, but it was the source of yet another dangerous adulterant. The beer served in many working-class pubs could be doctored with salt or vitriol, to make it more addictive to regular drinkers.[31] Though beer can provide important vitamins, it is rich in carbohydrate, which not only burdened its consumers with 'beer bellies' but seriously endangered their health, especially in the overall context of the diet just described. The relative absence of inhaled tobacco can have been one of the few modest bright spots in the people's health at the turn of the century, for the greater popularity of pipe as against cigarette smoking would have led to a lower ingestion of nicotine. Smoking amongst women was also relatively rare.

A lifetime of eating and drinking habits similar to those

described must have led to undernourishment and constipation, punctuated by summer diarrhoea, as general features. Salt, alcohol and cholesterol in abundance must have meant a precarious middle age, with an inevitable tendency towards digestive disorders, high blood-pressure and heart disease. It is hardly surprising that 97% of Salfordians failed to reach the modern pensionable age, even if they had been lucky enough to escape diphtheria in childhood and consumption as adults.

In an age lacking modern analgesics, opium and its derivatives laudanum and paregoric were widely used, with debilitating and sometimes fatal consequences. Modern researchers such as Michael J. Clarke have examined the extent of opium-taking in Victorian times, though in the nineteenth century drug dependency and death generally came through medical misuse rather than from recreational abuse. Until the Poisons Act of 1868, opium preparations were easily available over the counter, usually in the form of laudanum, which was a standard preparation of the opium alkaloid in alcohol.[32] In 1845, a police investigation in Bolton found fifty-four shops in the town openly selling opium, while in 1859 it was calculated that the equivalent of 1,410 mg of opium were consumed per person per year in England.[33] The 1868 Act changed the law only insofar as it required opium to be classed as a second schedule poison, sold only by pharmacists in bottles labelled 'poison', though anyone was still free to buy it. Even more remarkable, the 1868 Act did not deal with patent medicines containing opiates, so that if the patent medicine manufacturer complied with the law and put the threeha'penny 'government stamp' on his bottle, he could even purvey the drug as an unnamed ingredient in his preparation. Not until the Dangerous Drugs Act of 1920 was the law more effectively tightened to curb the easy sale of the drug and bring it under better control. After 1921, preparations containing more than 0.2% opium were available only by prescription. Before the launch of aspirin in the Edwardian period, and some of its newly isolated pharmaceutical relations, opium remained the universal domestic pain-killer, and could not without great hardship be removed from general access. Opiates were used for everything where pain, in whatever strength, had to be mitigated, including toothache, headache, internal disorders, insomnia and terminal illness.[34]

Proprietary baby-soothers such as 'Mother Winslow's Soothing Syrup' contained opium, while several coroner's juries sat on the deaths of babies whose mothers had given them opiates. An even cheaper baby-soother could be made by boiling the head of one single poppy flower in a small pan of water and giving it to the infant to drink.[35] Laudanum was sold as a bitter-tasting liquid, ten drops of which could put one out for the night or for ever, depending on a spectrum of variables which no housewife could know beforehand.

Opium derivatives were included in a wide variety of standard pharmaceutical preparations and patent medicines which were exempt from the 1868 Act. They were included in cough medicines, where their action suppressed the cough reflex and imparted a drugged doze to the bronchitic or consumptive.[36] Their calming action on the muscles of the digestive tract, combined with their analgesic properties, made them an essential ingredient for diarrhoea medicines, and the early formulas for 'Doctor Collis Browne's Mixture' relied heavily on opiates.[37]

Because of its pacifying action on the bowels, opium invariably caused constipation when administered as an analgesic, so that a mild purgative, such as rhubarb, would often be given with it. How many people became opium addicts through the persistent treatment of pains one will never know. How many more unwittingly became addicts to patent preparations which contained an undisclosed opium content is also impossible to ascertain, although the large amount of the drug in general circulation could go some way to explaining the Victorian obsession with poisons and good purges.

One looks in vain for a Victorian drug problem in the literature of the period that remotely parallels their concern with the 'demon drink'. Alcoholism, especially among the working classes, was a subject of grave concern to moralists, economists and national leaders, giving rise to the

Temperance Movement and legislation attempting to control access to drink. Opium-taking, however, aroused no condemnation and gave rise to no movements, though there was an awareness of its deleterious effects. Most probably this unconcern stemmed from an awareness of its medical side-effects, to which no congenital weakness of character or incipient criminality could be attributed, as with alcoholism.[38]

There are, however, references to euphoric, or 'kicks', drug-takers in both the medical and fictional annals of the period. Sheer economics, for instance, made it clear that one could get 'high' cheaper on a carefully-regulated dose of laudanum in tea or coffee than on beer. Laudanum cost about 8d for a one-fluid-ounce bottle, a half-dram (or 1/16) of which would give an inexperienced taker a 'lift' before dozing off, though a regular user needed more. Even so, one could forget one's troubles many times over on a shilling bottle, whereas it could cost the same amount to get drunk once in a public house.

'Recreational' or euphoric opium-taking was not uncommon in the mill towns of the north, especially before 1868, where for women it sometimes formed an alternative to the public house. The 'high' which opium was capable of imparting must have helped many people through the exhausting hours of the working day, not to mention cheap pleasure at night. The opium could be taken either in liquid form, or else smoked. John Barton, in Elizabeth Gaskell's *Mary Barton, a tale of Manchester Life* (1848), relied on the drug in times of stress:

'He had hesitated between the purchase of a meal or opium, and had chosen the latter, for its use had become a necessity to him. He wanted it to relieve him from the terrible depression its absence occasioned.'[39]

The mother of Eppie, the adopted daughter of George Eliot's handloom weaver *Silas Marner* (1861), had also died from the complications of opium addiction, while Conan Doyle's Sherlock Holmes (himself a cocaine addict) had an encounter in a low opium den in *The Man with the Twisted*

Lip (1891).[40] Laudanum was also used as a suicidal agent, being noted by many coroner's juries as well as by Robert Tressell in *The Ragged Trousered Philanthropists* (1914). By the first decade of the twentieth century, laudanum was becoming more difficult to purchase in lethal quantities, for when Tressell's character, Owen, was contemplating suicide for himself and his family, he soliloquised on how to obtain a large enough quantity:

> 'It would not be impossible to find some pretext for buying some laudanum: one could buy several small quantities at different shops until one had sufficient.'[41]

In none of these instances, either in reality or in fiction, is the drug user regarded as a social pariah like the contemporary alcoholic or the modern junkie, but as an object of pity. Why the Victorians regarded the drug addict more kindly than the alcoholic would be a fertile line of research.

Soon after cocaine came into medical use in the early 1880s, and heroin in the late 1890s, both were found to be highly addictive, though not until both had been championed as possible wonder drugs capable, amongst other things, of breaking opium addiction. The moral innocence of the addict is perhaps best summed up in that fictitious and perennially popular Victorian figure, Sherlock Holmes. Who, after all, in our own day could hope to write stories for family papers about a hero who was a cocaine user, disliked women, and shared a flat with a bachelor friend? Though Sherlock Holmes was hardly a working-class figure, his popularity, from the 1880s onwards, tells us much about the indulgence with which the Victorians could treat the drug user.

Though few people who provided me with information of a personal character mentioned anything directly dating back to the 'deregulated' days of opium, there was a clear remembrance of 'lodnum', 'knock-out drops' and 'sleeping draughts' passed on from their own parents. While the basic ingredients were becoming harder to purchase over the counter, opiate preparations still coloured the memories of a later generation.

These, therefore, were the hazards against survival with which the late Victorian housewife hoped to do battle, armed with a repertoire of empirical medical procedures, a bottle of laudanum, and, *in extremis*, the sixpenny doctor on his bicycle. What is astonishing, however, is the diversity of sources whence this folk medical repertoire derived, which for the majority of the population in 1900 still provided the overall context in which the people's health was conceived.

2

An immemorial tradition

It is a matter of no small wonder that mothers in Edwardian Manchester were still passing on to their daughters a concept of health and disease which would not have been out of place in the Athens of Plato: that people whose education was unlikely to have risen beyond the rudimentary 'three Rs', and who had never so much as heard of classical antiquity, should, by cultural osmosis, have imbibed some its most profound concepts. This is the root of the vernacular or oral tradition which lies at the heart of the Medicine of the People.

My own fascination with the subject dates from my teens in the mid - 1960s, in a family richly stocked with Victorians. My maternal grandparents were born in 1891 and 1892 respectively, and I had clear memories of a recently deceased paternal grandmother who had been born in 1872. From aunts and uncles – most of whom had been married before 1914 – and their equally aged friends and callers, I in turn came to pick up the tradition. As most of them lived on well into the 1970s and some into the mid-1980s, and as my interest in their lore came to crystallise, I had plenty of opportunities to verify details.

Health and sickness were always lively subjects of discussion, and from childhood onwards I had been familiar with references to hot blood, weak brains, constipation, purges, tight fits, and the 'swealing away' of illness, in remembered snippets of adult conversation. I knew that sulphur was a tonic, that herbs were good, and 'chemics' (chemicals) bad, and that the emotionally unstable or dull-witted should be kept out of moonlight to avoid being 'mooned'.

My grandfather was the possessor of a natural history lore, acquired no doubt from his fellow gardeners and pigeon-fanciers, that in retrospect was reminiscent of the medieval bestiaries or Pliny's *Historia Naturalis* of the first century A.D.[1] Until his dying day, in 1984, he maintained that nature was composed of hierarchies of sevens. There were seven 'true' flowers, seven 'true' herbs, seven 'true' stones, and the like. He spoke unwittingly of the four classical elements – earth, water, air and fire – and conceived of such phenomena as combustion and electricity as the action of vital forces in nature.[2] Electricity, he stated – and most of his male contemporaries and relatives agreed – had no master, coming as it did from the sky. No matter how many machines mankind invented for it to operate, people would always get electrocuted, for nature could not be bridled. I remember my father, born in 1907, quoting with a smile the doom-warning of a Clifton sage of his youth who claimed that man's attempts to harness nature's forces would 'goo and goo till they goo ore't'top'. Nature was a jealous mistress and the fate of Prometheus awaited those who presumed too much. One might suggest that the ancestral dread of a later generation has come to be focused on the use of atomic energy.

My grandfather received little formal education, going to work in 1903, at the age of twelve; however, he possessed a lively intellect and curiosity that could have taken him far had it been trained. It was this lively intellect, surviving into his nineties, which never ceased to amaze me with the world it encompassed. What I also recall from my childhood is that there were realms of knowledge for men, and others for women. My grandfather was the expert on scientific and philosophical issues, whereas it was my grandmother and aunts who offered judgement on medical matters. One is left to assume that one body of knowledge pertaining to plants, animals, minerals and weather was a male expertise, while matters relating to babies, nursing and the virtues of foodstuffs was a female one; though none of it was exclusive, and could be talked of by both sexes.

I gained my introduction to this broad medical and natural historical tradition no doubt as they did, by hearing it in conversation. Very soon, however, I came to deride it as superstitious nonsense and a collection of old wives' tales, quite out of keeping with what I was being taught at school and the elementary science books which I read for pleasure. Only in my mid-twenties, when as an historian of science I had become familiar with the academic scientific and medical ideas of the ancient Greeks, did I realise the connection. It was, of course, a tradition extending well beyond the bounds of my elderly family, and formed the fabric of a belief system common to a generation and its predecessors, who had learned what they knew by word of mouth.

This folk medical tradition was not thought of by its adherents as an articulated body of knowledge. When I came to ask people how they believed it to work or from where it derived, nothing could be offered. Though I could recognise within it the Greek doctrine of the humours, the astrological doctrine of signatures and the special properties of heat, blood, oils and purges, it lacked any coherent physiological basis. It was, indeed, the tail-end of an immemorial tradition, of which the precepts still remained, while the reasons had long since been forgotten. What I wish to do in this chapter is to look at how the ancient academic medical tradition evolved its concepts and procedures in the classical world, and how it came to form the basis of a vernacular tradition which still extends into the present century.

Medicine as a rational, systematic study based on cause and effect – as opposed to an irregular collection of recipes and empirical rules of thumb – dates back to the ancient Greeks. Whether the Greeks 'invented' rational medicine or developed it from earlier Egyptian traditions is hard to ascertain, though what we do know is that they were the first to organise it into a formal body of learning with rules, principles and procedures that were written down.[3]

Their first major writer was Hippocrates, subsequently known as the 'father of medicine', who was born on the island of Cos around 480 B.C. Hippocrates wrote on fevers, disease classification and therapeutic procedures, and compiled accurate case histories which stressed attention to the patient's physical symptoms, rather than possible occult or magical causes of disease.[4]

In classical Greece, medicine was viewed not just as a curative art, but as part of a wider understanding of man and the natural world, with its roots in philosophy.[5] Interested as they were in the cause and effect of 'the nature of things', the ancient Greeks attempted to classify the principles which moved all nature, including the health of mankind. This philosophy was grounded in a number of seemingly self-evident principles, centred on the existence of four elements, earth, water, air and fire. The intermixing of these elements caused all change in nature, and with them, the quintessential properties of the elements: cold, wet, dry and hot.[6]

The human body, likewise, contained its four parallel components, the four humours, which were also related to the elements and qualities. The four humours comprised Black Bile (Earth = cold and dry), Yellow Bile (Fire = hot and dry), Blood (Air = hot and wet) and Phlegm (Water = cold and wet).[7] The whole of classical philosophy placed great stress upon balance and all things being in their correct places – what Aristotle in the fourth century B.C. came to call the 'middle way'.

When this natural symmetry was disturbed, chaos ensued. When the four elements of nature were put out of balance, storm, earthquake and disaster followed; and when one of the bodily humours usurped the place of another, disease resulted. Though an astute Greek doctor would take the pulse, look at the complexion and inquire into the symptoms of his patient, he would do this with the end of discovering which humour had got out of place. Did the patient have a hot, cold, moist or dry disease, and in precisely what way were the humours 'compounded' in the particular case in question? Not only disease, but also character, was humoral in origin, for no two healthy people had precisely the same balance of humours. The humours gave people their individual temperaments: the Choleric (Yellow Bile = hot-tempered), Bilious (Black Bile = melancholy or dark-tempered), Sanguine (Blood = vital, balanced) and Phlegmatic (Phlegm = cool).[8]

Everybody had a mixture of humours within them, though one usually predominated, to produce individual features of personality. Different temperaments had predispositions towards particular disorders: for instance, persons with too much Black Bile (Melancholy) were likely to be depressive, whereas their contrary type was the Sanguine. The humoral classification of human types, and their related inclinations, underlay much of the literature of the Renaissance, when it was still in vogue. It interpenetrates the motivations of many of Shakespeare's characters, while Ben Jonson's *Every Man in his Humour* (1598) speaks for itself.[9]

In addition to the humours, later classical medicine also held that there were three spirits in the body: the Natural Spirits in the liver, the Vital Spirits in the heart, and the Animal Spirits in the brain. These were seen as vital forces within the body that had relations with the functions of nourishment, vital heat, emotion and thought.[10]

Not until the seventeenth century did doctors know that the blood circulated around the body. According to the earlier classical doctrines, blood was thought to be 'concocted' in the liver from nutriments conveyed from the stomach, thereby placing great importance on the role of the liver as the source of life-giving blood. The liver also infused the new blood with Natural Spirits, and these, with the blood, rose up into the heart. In the heart, life-giving air was blown into the blood by the lungs (which acted like bellows), to impregnate it with the Vital Spirits.[11] Effervescing out of the heart, and warmed by it, the blood was thought to enter the *veins* (not the arteries) which conveyed it to the limbs in a series of ebbing movements that were thought to be similar to the tides. In the limbs, the blood was turned into flesh and thereby imparted warmth and vitality. One grew thin and weak when one did not eat because the blood diminished in quantity and quality and contained less nutriment, while the consumption of infected, bland or strong foods gave rise to sickness, moderation or strength in the flesh. This was why coal-heavers needed plenty of beef and why babies and invalids could take only milk.

Some of the blood, which was thought to have passed through the septum wall in the heart, was conveyed into the head where it generated the Animal Spirits in a net of blood vessels at the base of the brain, known as the *rete mirabile* or 'wonderful network'. These Spirits were cold by nature, and were believed to control the intellect and the nervous system. The brain also served the function of a cooling plant for the body, which moderated the excessive temperatures generated

in the furnace-like heart. Aristotle drew attention to the heart
as the fundamental organ of the body, though he saw it as a
furnace rather than a pump.[12] Like a furnace, and aerated
through the pulmonary blood vessels by the lungs, it refined
the original crude blood that rose up from the liver, imparting
life-giving innate heat and burning off the 'dregs', which
were exhaled from the mouth as bad breath. The cool brain,
on the other hand, prevented over-heating. Aristotle also
considered that the heart was the seat of the soul, sensitivity
and feeling, while the brain was the source of dispassionate
calculation. We still preserve this way of thinking when we
speak of people who are warm-hearted, or who possess kind
hearts, in the same way as we speak of other types of people
as cool-headed.

One can easily see how this conception of physiology –
which held academic sway from before the time of Christ
down to the seventeenth century A.D. – exerted a profound
influence on how the body and its processes were imagined.
It left its mark on language, and permeated the English tongue
from Chaucer to Milton (not to mention the languages of
Europe), and still lies at the heart of many commonplaces of
everyday speech. We still describe people as cool-headed,
warm-hearted, bilious, choleric and phlegmatic. We are
sometimes 'liverish' when too much alcohol has 'agitated'
our blood, while spontaneous, happy people have 'light'
hearts and plenty of 'vital spirits'. Who has not encountered
the truism that young people are 'hot-headed', while old ones
have 'thick blood' which cools like an emulsifying oil with
the passing years?[13] Though we may no longer think of the
ageing process in terms of the same seven divisions as in
Shakespeare's *As You Like It* (1599), these disconnected ideas
still underpin everyday conversation about the human
condition.[14]

Classical medicine approached disease from the vantage
point of the gardener or nurse, rather than of the engineer.
The body was a delicate collection not of organs but of
abstract properties, which often had strong moral overtones.
Health lay in balance, nourishment, and aiding nature. The
body's natural tendency was to get better, for by the same

logic which argued that teeth were made to eat with and not to ache, so the 'good' function of the body would naturally re-assert itself as soon as the 'bad' invading agents were removed from it. The body was to be tended like a garden, with gentleness, over a long period of time. Once damaged, health had to be gently nursed 'back into it', in the way that a storm-wrecked garden had to be restored to its 'natural' order. Time and patience were seen as the great healers, aided by the correct diet to suit the injured humours, and by the application of mild herbal medicine. Classical medicine – at least in its practical therapeutics – was an art and not a science, depending not upon diagnostic technology or clever mechanical procedures, but upon the shrewd intuition of a wise and experienced practitioner.

Though dealing in the actions of relatively vague, non-physical processes, classical medicine nonetheless had a firm intellectual basis. Its concern with taxonomy and classification had developed an elaborate system of diagnostics and prognostics, in which the humours, their hot and cold properties, affinities, and reactions with food and drugs, had been minutely worked out. This system had formed the curriculum of the medical faculties of medieval Oxford, Paris and Bologna, and created the concept of the university-trained physician with a doctor's degree. No one, moreover, who had received a formal medical training up to as late as 1850 could have obtained his degree without imbibing at least something of this tenacious tradition, for classical medicine did not so much die as slowly fade away over some three centuries.[15] Specific components of its repertoire, such as the humours, were called into question and superseded little by little, yet its philosophical foundations, rooted in the reverence for life and the Hippocratic Oath, are still hot topics of debate on such contemporary questions as abortion, the switching off of life-support machines, and medical ethics.

The new approach to medicine which grew up in the sixteenth century did not deny the precepts of the classical tradition, but drew attention to different priorities. The key to the new medicine of the Renaissance was anatomy. Without an accurate knowledge of the body's structure, the healing art could never escape from its immemorial limitations. Anatomists such as Andreas Vesalius and Hieronymus Fabricius ab Aquapedente in middle and late sixteenth-century Padua drew attention to the body's organs rather than its humours.[16] The Englishman William Harvey created the basis of modern physiology when in 1628 he discovered, through an exemplary series of experiments, that the blood actually circulated around the body, being pumped by the heart into the arteries, and returning to it via the veins.[17]

Inspired as many of these men and their seventeenth-century successors were by contemporary discoveries in the physical sciences of mechanics and astronomy, it came to be argued that, if the Universe was an exact machine which followed rational laws, then so should the human body. After all, the same God had designed and made them both. Between 1550 and 1700 a series of discoveries were made about the functioning of the human body, along with its comparison to the creatures of the animal kingdom. In France, René Descartes discovered the muscle reflex and the body's involuntary functions; while in Italy, in 1661 Marcello Malpighi demonstrated the microscopic blood circulation and the basis of embryology.[18] In England, Thomas Willis began the scientific study of the human brain, and Robert Hooke and John Mayow disclosed the chemical basis of respiration.[19] At every turn, the body was coming to be seen as an elaborate self-acting machine, amenable to experimental investigation, and more closely resembling the watch in its basic principles than a system of philosophical hierarchies.

The creators of this new medicine stressed what we would now call its scientific foundations, optimistically believing that once the anatomical and physiological structures of the body had been described, and specific diseases ascribed to mechanical malfunctions, then it could be repaired, at least in principle, like a defective watch. This was to form the scientific foundation of the medicine of the modern West, though for its first two or three centuries it was capable of curing pitifully few diseases and alleviating little suffering at the practical therapeutic level. These early medical scientists studied, weighed and measured the body in the same way as their colleagues in astronomy measured the heavens; however, their knowledge gave them no more power over disease than the astronomers' knowledge enabled them to stop the Sun in the sky.

Yet whenever these new doctors dealt with actual diseases amongst living people, they fell back into the classical therapeutics in which they had been originally trained. They may have known that a patient with advanced tuberculosis was suffering from severely damaged lungs, rather than an excess of cold humours, but there was nothing they could have done about it. Knowing what one would find in the ensuing post mortem might represent a triumph of scientific procedure, but it was of precious little value to the patient. In consequence, the doctor came to work within two medical cultures: scientific medicine which told him how the body worked as a mechanism; and time-honoured classical procedures to use on the sick. That these two approaches applied separately to the living and the dead can have done little to enhance the status of the profession in real terms.

It was not until the nineteenth century that the growing corpus of scientific knowledge about the human body began to make a serious impact on disease. Jenner's discovery of smallpox vaccination in 1798 was important, along with the realisation by 1860 that clean water and good sanitation could limit the spread of cholera, typhoid and other epidemic diseases.[20] Thus from the 1840s began the growing torrent of scientific medical advances: chloroform anaesthesia in 1847, antiseptic surgery in 1865, the identification of specific disease bacteria from 1870 onwards, X-rays in 1895, blood-group typing from 1900, and the first 'magic bullet' drug, Paul Ehrlich's Salvarsan 606, for the treatment of syphilis, in 1904. The scientific instrumentation of medicine likewise began to develop, with the stethoscope between 1816 and 1852, the hypodermic syringe in 1853, the clinical thermometer by 1860 and the sphygmomanometer to measure blood pressure by the 1890s, and the advancement of clinical photography.[21] Keeping pace with these new applications of science to practical medicine came the sudden and continuous

Asclepius with his Caduceus wand offers relief to a sick Victorian lady. Alfred Fennings' late Victorian patent medicine advertising perfectly captures the image of classical medicine and the chord which its supposed ancient wisdom was expected to strike in the popular mind. *Fennings' Everybody's Doctor: or, when ill, how to get well* (undated booklet, *post* 1863), front cover. (Author's collection.)

rise in life expectancy, from about forty years in 1840 to fifty-three in 1911, seventy in 1950 and over seventy-five today. [22]

Within the culture of early modern Europe, from the seventeenth century onwards, medicine came to develop two distinct approaches towards its human subjects. This was a parting of the ways between the older classical and newer scientific traditions. In practice, it tended to mean that an educated person would have at least some familiarity with the basic assumptions of scientific medicine, as part of his general knowledge of nature, and would appreciate its aspirations and methods.

On the other hand, however, the uneducated remained unfamiliar with the new medicine and science in most of their forms, and while they had received no actual training in classical medicine, they had nonetheless picked up a rich, if disorganised, smattering of its general ideas from the prevailing vernacular culture. This, indeed, represented that

Asclepius with his ancient Caduceus wand of serpent and staff – the classical emblem of the physician – staving off Death's arrow with his healing cup, before a bewhiskered Victorian patient. *Fennings' Everybody's Doctor*, back cover. (Author's collection.)

diffuse body of ideas which penetrated deep into the minds and language of the unlearned to form the Medicine of the People.

Precisely how the elaborate conceptions of classical medicine, as they would have been taught in the lecture halls of the late medieval universities, left their Latin and Greek roots to form a popular tradition is of considerable interest, and I believe it took place in several stages. That classical medicine was already an established possession of the fourteenth-century middle classes is borne out by Chaucer, whose writings make extensive reference to its precepts. Though not a physician himself, Chaucer was a man who had probably attended Oxford University, and was certainly widely read in the sciences of his day. In *The Nun's Priest's Tale* in particular, he displays a detailed knowledge of humoral physiology, and discusses whether dreams are omens, or simply the products of digestive irregularities.[23]

The *Canterbury Tales*, indeed, not only contains abundant references to humours and their attributes, but also shows knowledge of medical astrology and the supposed influence of the heavens upon plants and animals. While intended originally for a courtly though not an academic audience, the *Tales* soon won great popularity, and might be regarded as reflecting ideas in current circulation in the 1380s. Chaucer writes of an essentially bourgeois world of merchants, physicians, men of law and rich widows, and one wonders how the ideas common amongst such people would have penetrated to the landless peasantry, who lacked the means and leisure to travel. Unfortunately, there are few indications of what the really poor thought in Chaucer's time; and while one may feel that a character like the Canon's Yeoman, with his impressive knowledge of alchemy, came from a more humble background than most of the other pilgrims, he had once been an independent farmer who had foolishly squandered his money in financing the gold-making schemes of his master.[24]

Two centuries later, by the time of Shakespeare, there is plenty of evidence to suggest that classical medical ideas were in wide circulation across society at large, for many of his plays contain references to them. Though many of these plays were originally intended for courtly performances, Shakespeare's popular success, by the time of his death in 1616, meant that he could not be pitching his causal agencies too far above the heads of the groundlings. Shakespeare uses humoral physiology to explain the make-up and dominant traits of many of his characters. When, in *The Merchant of Venice*, Bassanio is choosing his casket, the chorus ponders whether, when we make random guesses, we are swayed by our cool heads or passionate hearts:

'Tell me where is fancy bred,
Or in the heart or in the head?
How begot, how nourished?'[25]

Fancy, to an Elizabethan, meant imagination, which is an important factor in choosing, and bore directly on the physiological ideas of Aristotle and Galen.

When Benedick has toothache in *Much Ado About Nothing*, Leonarto speculates whether it is caused by a worm or a humour; while the reason for Othello's lack of jealousy, itself a humoral relative of Black Bile, is that the Sun 'drew all such humours from him'.[26] Temperaments are often characterised in humoral terms by Shakespeare: the conceited Don Adriano has a 'lofty humour' in *Love's Labours Lost*, while England herself is beset with 'the inundation of mistempered humours' and medicines have to be applied to the Body Politic itself in *King John*.[27] Shakespeare sums up the humoral theory beautifully in *Romeo and Juliet*, where Friar Laurence gives Juliet the drug which will simulate death:

'When presently through thy veins shall run
a cold and drowsy humour, which shall seize
each Vital Spirit; for no pulse shall keep
his natural progress, but surcease to beat;
no warmth, no breath, shall testify thou livest.'[28]

By the time of Shakespeare's established success after 1600, however, there had already been published a substantial range of books which clearly purported to place a knowledge of 'physicke' within the reach of the poor. Influenced, quite probably, by the Reformation, several Tudor medical men came to condemn the exclusiveness of their profession, and regarded it as a Christian duty to make their knowledge accessible to the poor and non-Latin readers. One of the first to do this was Andrew Boorde, a former monk and medical graduate of Montpellier, who also served Henry VIII as a diplomat. In Boorde's *Dietry* (1542) and *Breviary of Health* (1547), he laid down the rules of health in simple English, couched within the broad assumptions of the classical medicine in which he was trained. Many of these rules might strike us today as little more than common-sense hygiene, as when in the *Dietry*, Boorde inveighs against the insanitary practice of 'pyssing in chimnies';[29] however, we should bear in mind that such an act would not have seemed so obviously unhygienic to a subject of King Henry.

Boorde's books were short, simply written, and aimed at a non-specialist readership, and many physicians and medical men came to follow suit over the next century. William Bullein's *Government of Healthe* (1558) and *Bulwarke of Health* (1579) presented medicine in English, while the title of Thomas Brassbridge's *Poor Man's Jewel, That is to say a Treatise on the Pestilence* (1578) speaks for itself.[30] Some of these popularisers, moreover, while academically educated men, confessed to possessing no formal medical qualifications. Such a person was Sir Thomas Elyot who, in the Preface to his *Castel of Helth* (1541), admits to not being a doctor, though widely read in the works of Galen, Dioscorides, Hippocrates and other classical medical writers.[31] In many ways, one might see this 'poor man's physicke' culminating in the *Herbal* and *Compleat English Physician* of Dr Nicholas Culpeper in 1652. Writing at a time when the English Revolution was upsetting the traditional privileges of the Royal College of Physicians, Culpeper produced a work which was destined to become one of the best-sellers in the history of popular medicine. Culpeper believed not only in humoral physiology, but also the astrological 'virtues' of many plants and medicinal substances, which had to be gathered, prepared and administered at the correct celestial aspect. Though Culpeper's was not the first herbal to be available in English, having been preceded by those of John Gerard and others, it was to become one of the most influential.[32]

The *British Library Catalogue* lists fifty editions of Culpeper's *English Physician* between 1652 and 1863, with several more in the twentieth century; and the work is still in print.[33] Culpeper's *English Midwife* also enjoyed great popularity, and has recently been reissued under the title *The Book of Birth*.[34] Another work of great influence was the *Regimen Sanitatis Salerni*, ascribed to the medieval writer Arnold of Villa Nova, of which there were numerous Latin editions by 1550. English translations began to appear in 1528, including Thomas Paynel's in 1541, and the work was to go through ten English editions by 1649.[35] The *Regimen* conveyed the principles of classical (and medieval) medicine, along with its rules for diet and exercise, the value of moderation, and similar procedures.[36] Sir Thomas Elyot's *Castel of Helth* confirmed its precepts in English, and was itself to go through ten editions by 1610.

Although all of these works, along with a variety of others, were to place the concepts of classical medicine before the vernacular English reader, it would be incorrect to assume that they necessarily reached the market for which they were intended – the poor. Impoverished people, after all, had little spare money to spend on what would still have been relatively costly books. While evidence suggests that something in the region of 40–50% of the Tudor population was literate to some extent, and these books would have been linguistically accessible to people capable of reading the English *Bible, Prayer Book* or Foxe's *Martyrs*, they would still have been over-priced for those who needed them most.[37]

One major vehicle that carried the precepts of classical science and medicine to the poor, however, would have been astrological almanacks. These were little books, usually containing around thirty pages of small print, on which there was a wide diversity of information about astrology, medicine, agriculture, the weather, and so on. They first appeared in England during the latter years of Henry VlIl's reign, and grew to a flood of popularity under Elizabeth and the early Stuarts, with as many as two to three dozen individual writers producing their published contributions annually.[38] Almanacks gave excellent value for their price of between 2d and 6d per copy. They were hawked around by pedlars and read out in taverns and by firesides so that their contents often penetrated into the world of the illiterate. That they were widely spread through Tudor society, and purchased and read by working people, is again borne out by Shakespeare. In *A Midsummer Night's Dream*, when the mechanicals are waiting to pick a moonlit night on which to rehearse their play, it is Bottom who calls for an almanack, and Quince the joiner who obligingly has one at hand.[39] Some of the most comic and absurd figures invented by Shakespeare therefore include in their ranks at least one man who can read and who buys cheap books.

SOUTHWARK COLLEGE LIBRARY
SURREY DOCKS CENTRE
DRUMMOND ROAD
LONDON SE16 4EE

Many almanack writers claimed medical credentials. Some used titles such as 'physician' or 'practitioner of physicke'; John Securis of Salisbury, for instance, styled himself as 'Master of Art and Physicke' in 1579.[40] Even if these men only used precepts borrowed from earlier medical popularisers, such as Boorde, rather than from Aristotle or Hippocrates direct, they nonetheless fulfilled an invaluable service in passing on simplified components of learned medicine to ordinary people, which must have gone a long way towards amplifying the Medicine of the People.

It might be said, therefore, that by 1400 one finds indications from Chaucer that classical medicine had left the lecture hall and entered the possession of the middle classes. Though it may have (and probably had) already passed into the everyday parlance of working people by the same date, we do not have solid evidence for this until the sixteenth century. By 1600, however, it had firmly arrived at what might be called street level, as we find from its usage by Shakespeare and other contemporary playwrights, from medical popularisers, and from the pervasive power of almanacks.

Yet by the time that popularised classical medicine had entered general parlance, the most forward-looking of doctors were coming to question its principles, and to evolve new conceptions of health based upon anatomy and experimental science. The scientific movement of the seventeenth century had strong medical interests, and the 'reform of physicke' had become one of its ambitions. In the *New Atlantis* (1628), Sir Francis Bacon spoke of the need to reform and improve medicine as one of the priorities of the new science, and several modern scholars have drawn attention to the momentum which this movement had gained by 1660.[41] By seeing the human body as a divinely created mechanism within the greater mechanism of the natural world, the new medicine took a fresh direction. After the work of Harvey – who demonstrated that the blood moves around the body under the influence of a pumping heart – and the new chemical physicians, the older doctrines of humours and spirits seemed less convincing. By the eighteenth century the body was coming to be seen as a collection of pneumatic, hydraulic and chemical systems, especially in the wake of Hermann Boerhaave at Leiden and William Cullen in Edinburgh.[42] Although these new 'scientific' doctors, as noted earlier, still used the language and ideas of classical medicine when it suited, their approach to physiology had become fundamentally different from that of colleagues of a century before, whereas the approach of an early Tudor doctor would still have been classical.

For those persons who had received a learned education, or who moved socially amongst the new doctors, a new attitude was bound to develop. One of the earliest of these educated laymen to grasp the analogy of scientific ideas to medicine was the philosopher Thomas Hobbes, who also happened to be a friend of Dr Harvey. In his *Leviathan* (1651), Hobbes characterised man as a machine, whose organs were like the 'springs and wheels' of a watch:

'For what is the heart but a spring; and the nerves as so many strings; and the joynts but so many wheeles, giving motion to the whole body?' [43]

Hobbes saw life itself as an ongoing state of motion among parts, and death as a cessation of the same. Such opinions obviously made Hobbes a notorious figure, though they indicate the way in which lay ideas were moving when it came to looking at the human body. Though Hobbes' failure to discuss man in religious terms isolated him as an extreme thinker, one finds that by the late seventeenth and early eighteenth centuries the educated classes were coming to differ substantially in their views about man and the natural world from their servants and tenants.

In addition to the power of oral continuity among the uneducated, there was a line of published works which both maintained and reinforced the older medical tradition. One of the most influential of these works was John Wesley's *Primitive Physick* (1747). This book, which claimed to be 'for the easy cure of most diseases', was written by an educated man who clearly lamented the way in which academic medicine was moving. In the Preface he re-emphasised a theory of disease rooted in original sin and for which God had granted relief by means of herbs and simples:

> 'But in process of time, men of philosophical [scientific] turn were not satisfied with this ... They examined the human body in all its parts; the nature of the flesh, veins, arteries, nerves; the structure of the brain, heart, lungs, stomach, bowels ... Men of learning began to set experience aside to set physick upon hypothesis... As theories increased, simple medicines were more disregarded, till in course of years the greater part of them were forgotten, at least in the politer nations... Medical books were immensely multiplied till at length physick became an abstruse science, quite out of the reach of ordinary men.'[44]

Wesley's intention was to give physick back to ordinary people.

While Wesley had interests in aspects of the new science, such as electricity, his essentially theological explanation of disease made him regard its application to medicine as limited and even dangerous. By reiterating the 'virtues' of simples, and publishing a book of their uses, he was continuing the Tudor tradition of the gentleman acting as the poor man's advocate, who condemned the pretensions and exclusiveness of his social equals.

Primitive Physick was to remain a regular seller for a century after its first publication. The *British Library Catalogue* lists thirteen editions by 1768, and thirty-two by 1828, with further printings in 1832, 1846 and 1847. Though the British Library records no further accession until the modern editions of 1958 and 1960, this should not be interpreted as indicating the book's disappearance from circulation. *Primitive Physick* also went through American printings. What is important, however, is the effect which this little book, written by a major religious leader, must have had on ordinary people, especially when one remembers how deeply Methodism penetrated into the English working class.[45]

36

A work which might arguably have been even more influential in anchoring classical or traditional medical ideas into the popular mind was that remarkable compilation known as *Aristotle's Works*. Based loosely on the authentic *De Generatione Animalium*[46] (*On the Generation of Animals*) of Aristotle, composed around 340 B.C., and one of the earliest surviving treatises on mammal embryology, the pseudo-Aristotelian *Works* made their appearance towards the end of the seventeenth century. The book constituted a genre publication, anonymously compiled and endlessly reissued, with changes to suit prevailing fashions, until well within living memory. The *British Library Catalogue* records the survival of twenty-two copies from editions issued between 1777 and 1905, only twelve of which carry precise publication dates. The rest were left undated by the printers and received *circa* dates from the British Library, depending on internal means of dating, such as typeface style and watermarks.[47]

Aristotle's Works had the reputation of being a sex manual – or more precisely, a book for newly-weds, pregnant women and nursing mothers. In an age when information on these subjects was virtually unobtainable to all but the medically trained, it was a 'secret book', and to be kept away from children. The prevailing ignorance of the average woman concerning accurate physiological information, indeed, was highlighted by Dr Henry Arthur Allbutt of Leeds, when he wrote in 1891:

'She has been brought up from her earliest years not to ask questions... She has been brought up in the grossest ignorance of her physical self, and the function of her own organs.'

The only place to which she could turn, therefore, said Dr Allbutt, was to old wives' tales, superstitions and 'books of the 'Aristotle' type'.[48] Allbutt was not the only individual concerned with informing women about their own bodies and health, for amongst others he was preceded in America by Dr Alice Bunker Stockham M.D., whose *Tokology: A Book for Every Woman* (Chicago, 1885) aimed to do just that. The heart of Dr Stockham's campaign, in fact, was to raise awareness of the harm done to women's uterine, abdominal and thoracic cavities by the late-Victorian fashion for tightly-laced corsets, and to advance the cause of 'Dress Reform' with its non-constricting garments.[49]

Aristotle's Works generally contained four (and sometimes more) sections, only two of which dealt with sexual matters: 'Aristotle's Masterpiece' and 'Experienced Midwife'. The rest of the book covered a wide range of general topics in medicine and natural history. In its entirety, the *Works* usually consisted of some three, four or more hundred pages of small print, maintaining its physical affinity with the almanack, though considerably thicker. Its explanations remained traditional and classical in form, and even well into the Victorian period made few concessions to developments in contemporary science.

From two sections of the *Works* generally known as 'The Family Physician' and 'Aristotle's Book of Problems', one can easily trace a system of medicine which had survived unchanged through the centuries and could well have come from the mouths of Shakespeare's characters. From a dated London edition of 1857 one finds that the blood is generated in the liver from food, thereafter passing into the veins, without reference to the arteries. Women are said to have thicker blood than men, because women are naturally colder than men, so that their blood curdles more easily.[50] The concepts of humoral physiology run through the entire book, and are often imparted by the classical 'question and answer' technique:

> Q. 'How many ways is the brain purged, and other hidden places of the body?'
> A. 'Four; the watery and gross humours are purged by the eyes, melancholy by the ears, choler by the nose, and phlegm by the hair.'[51]

A similar approach underlies the administration of medicines. A treatment for apoplexy (usually stroke, heart attack or paralysis) recommends 'take a man's skull prepared, powder of the roots of a male peony, of each an ounce and a half.' [52] The recommended man's skull was a pure piece of ancient sympathetic magic, for this referred to a substance called Usnea, a mould which grew on dead men's skulls, which was thought capable of stimulating life by contact with the bones of the dead.

This book made a major impression on ordinary folk well into the early twentieth century – a fact borne out by several contemporary references. The historian A.L. Rowse recollected it from his childhood in Edwardian Cornwall,[53] while Gracie Fields recalls it as a necessary ingredient in a hopeful spinster's trousseau in the Rochdale of the 1930s:

'One toilet set, one basinette,
Now I'm waiting for love to open up the door,
Got me *Aristotle's Works* and a case of eggs from Pearks,
ALL PACKED UP IN MY LITTLE BOTTOM
        DRAWER.'[54]

As a child, I can remember nods and winks at the mention of 'Harry Stotle', and whether or not he was in work!

Because of its sexual content, *Aristotle's Works* was not a 'respectable' book, though there were many Victorian domestic publications which helped to pass on aspects of the pre-scientific tradition in a less notorious way. This was true of many household hints books which contained medical advice where ancient and modern fragments could appear together. Such was the case with the popular *Consult Me*, the 1883 edition of which started by castigating the 'barbarous practices' of the allopathist (orthodox) physicians, and recommending 'mild' treatments using water and herbs.[55] Though entering into no physiological discussion and saying nothing about humours by name, its strong stress on botanical and water remedies places it in the same tradition as *Primitive Physick*, and harks back to Hippocrates' *Airs, Waters and Places*. [56]

Though many household books held to a very traditional line in their medical sections, it is important to notice that one of the most influential of such books ever to have been written did not. Isabella Beeton's *Book of Household*

Management (1869 edition) in its thirty-one-page section on 'The Doctor' discusses the best scientific medicine of the day. Written not only by Mrs Beeton herself, but with 'the aid of a gentleman of large professional experience', this section aims to deal with almost every medical emergency. The family medicine chest should contain antimony powder, spirits of nitre, calomel, various mineral and metallic drugs, opium, laudanum and a small set of surgical instruments. Precise details are given for how to 'bleed' a patient who has just had a stroke, along with how to prepare various pharmaceutical substances. There are no references to humours, balance, homeopathy or any of the classical elements found in publications intended to instruct the poor. On the other hand, it should not be forgotten that Mrs Beeton's book, with its advice on how to deal with servants and prepare banquets, aimed at a middle- and upper-class readership. The medical hints are essentially first-aid measures intended to be used while waiting for the doctor to arrive, rather than the forlorn hope of the poor. Her book highlights very clearly the different attitudes towards medicine found between the upper and lower classes of the mid- and late Victorian periods, and how money and education created different fundamental assumptions from those of the slum-dweller.[57]

At the opposite end of the scale, the world view of classical, or at least pre-scientific, medicine was firmly enshrined in the literature of patent medicines, especially when aimed at the less well-off. Many of those nineteenth-century firms such as Alfred Fennings which manufactured large quantities of patent medicines began to issue 'medical books' to promote their products. These books often went through an alphabetical list of complaints, in which they tried to explain the causes of most diseases, before saying how to cure them with a patent preparation. The tendency to explain both causes and cures in the language of traditional medicine indicates a shrewd awareness on the part of the promoter of how his potential readers and customers viewed their maladies. I shall be discussing these publications, and how they both inherited and helped to pass on the 'ancient way', when dealing with patent medicines in Chapter 4.

Whatever the precise route taken, it cannot be denied that many important features of ancient medicine were not only in oral circulation by the late nineteenth century, but were reinforced by the written word. It is also true that poverty, illiteracy and that savage segregation of classes which was part and parcel of industrialism forced the working classes of 1900 to inhabit a different medical and cultural world from that of their social betters. Yet this world owed astonishingly little to the new science, and with its traditional stress upon blood and bile, hot and cold, good and bad, enshrined an ancestry that passed back through Wesley to Boorde, and on to the immemorial fathers of European medicine.

3

The pathology of the people: a popular explanation for disease

The ways in which we think of disease and health affect us on many levels. Because illness is, in many respects, a mysterious process, it is hardly surprising that when encountered, it often produces irrational responses. It affects the way in which we use language, how we characterise what we feel is wrong with us and how, even today, we instinctively fall back into a curious mixture of world views when attempting to define it. We wish that pain would 'go away', we say that foolish people who run risks 'invite' infirmity, and that the unfortunate have 'got' something wrong with them. No matter how much, on our modern rational level, we know that disease is a functional disorder within the body, we still lapse back, when under stress, to earlier ways of thinking. In this earlier way of thinking, the body is a sovereign territory, analogous to the self, whereas disease is an external predator, lurking in the darkness, ready to catch us off guard, invade, and make us ill. It is, after all, a way of thinking vastly older than anything brought forth by modern science. It is fundamental to the manner in which disease was characterised in the Old Testament, while possession by and expulsion of invading demons lies at the heart of many of Christ's healing miracles in the Gospels.

Disease as a foreign agency, upsetting a balance within the body, not only brings us close to the modern-day practical application of classical medicine, but also to the idea of disease as the product of sin. Who has not heard of the mischief maker whose sickness or accident was said to have come from God, or the indigestion sufferer whose stomach was always 'out of balance'? These ways in which disease was explained and defined form what might be called a pathology of the people. Semi-subliminal as its use may be today, it still formed a clear pathology in 1900, and underlies most of the explanations encountered in my research.

The Medicine of the People contains a repertoire of truisms which relate directly to classical medical ideas as outlined in the last chapter, and one of the most central of these is concerned with blood. Just as blood formed the cornerstone for Aristotle, Galen and the other classical writers, so it was fundamental to the Victorian working class tradition. On the level of common parlance, this is hardly surprising when one thinks how central is the 'lifeblood' to continued existence. More important, however, are popular ideas of what blood is, and where it is thought to come from. Though I have not encountered any modern elderly person who spoke of blood as a 'humour', many were still willing to attribute most of the traditional humoral properties to it.

Most of the people with whom I spoke on the subject were unequivocal that blood was generated from the food we eat. My grandfather, among others, believed that it was generated in the liver, and that it was for this reason that one should take trouble to keep the liver and kidneys well cleansed. Patent 'liver salts' and 'liver pills' manufacturers were no doubt aware of this belief, and turned it to profitable ends. Beef was considered to produce the best blood, capable of strengthening and fortifying the flesh; the assumption being that the fluid was burnt up in the tissues rather than circulating around the entire body. Indeed, the classical doctrines of Galen, which saw the blood as a substance extracted from food which was burnt up in the limbs while generating heat and life, became so firmly entrenched into folk medicine that Harvey's discovery of the circulation seems to have made little impact outside the academic world.[1]

Blood also varied in temperature at different stages of life. Young blood was hot and nourishing, while old blood was cold and poor. Ageing itself was partly the result of the blood losing its sustaining power and going turgid.[2] The blood also varied between the sexes, men having relatively hotter blood than women, thereby explaining the old, albeit incorrect, belief that women were more prone to chills than were men. Indeed, this well-established folk belief in the innate temperature variations between men and women had a clear ancestry running back to the authentic Aristotle and other ancient writers. In classical medicine, with its love of balances and opposites, it was natural that the 'active' sex should be hot, and the 'passive' one cold; while in addition to their inherent coolness, women's overall temperature was kept low by menstruation.[3]

Many times have I heard nosebleeds characterised as 'nature's safety valve'. If the body, for whatever reason, generates too much blood, it can be disposed of via the nose, thereby 'purging the brain'. To a generation becoming vaguely aware of the relation between brain clots and strokes, as were the people of the early twentieth century, it seemed obvious that if the brain became engorged with blood, the nose was the best place from which to tap it. As nature's way, moreover, is always the right one, what could be more reasonable than to suppose that when excessive eating had made too much blood, the nose should automatically release it before damage could result?

Cuts incurred accidentally could also be a good thing in moderation, and in a healthy person should be allowed to bleed on awhile before being staunched. One could thereby allow any 'badness', which was likely to cause infection, to drain away, while a good 'bleed' could do one good, and make room for fresh blood to be generated. Many elderly blood donors have claimed that quite apart from the benefit bestowed on the sick by blood donation, the loss also benefited the donor. It is interesting to think how close we are here to the ancient practice of phlebotomy, or blood-letting, which in traditional medicine was a classic device for regulating the body's balance.[4]

Blood also influenced temperament and heredity, though this was a classical idea which retained an important role in orthodox medicine until the discovery of chromosomes in the twentieth century. Even reputable scientists like Charles Darwin, and his evolutionist cousin Francis Galton, saw blood as the hereditary agent and cross-transfused the blood of black rabbits and white rabbits to test the hypothesis in an attempt to isolate its genetic agent.[5] Seventeenth-century doctors had also experimented with blood transfusion, as a way of treating the insane, and of producing personality change.[6] Their argument had been that if the blood was the causal agent of temperament (rather than discarded astrology), then one could pacify the mad by injecting them with the blood of young lambs, and invigorate the impotent with the blood of goats or stallions. With such an academic lineage so recently behind it, it is hardly surprising that the belief that character was 'in the blood' should have survived so long on a popular level. The belief that certain families contained 'bad blood' was axiomatic, and such a lineage could account for criminality, alcoholism and madness.[7]

Though less central than blood, bile and phlegm also had their significance. 'Biliousness' was a common complaint, and one still frequently spoken of. In traditional physiology bile was believed to be generated in the spleen, and I have been told of ill-tempered people who were 'splenetic,' or had 'too much spleen'. Of course, this ancient world view began to phase in with a better knowledge of scientific physiology by the middle of the twentieth century, and people now make references to their 'bile duct' or gall bladder. This association is hardly surprising when one remembers that bile was also seen as the bitter 'gall', generated in certain parts of the body, the excess or defect of which contributed both to overall temperament and to an individual's proneness to disease. 'Bile Beans', which the author can still remember being sold in the corner shops of the north until recent times, were originally intended to purge and regulate the awkward 'bilious' humour.

Phlegm was the cold, wet humour of classical physiology, the root cause of most languishing, life-draining diseases, when possessed in excess. Its causal character still survives as the patron substance of bad colds, pneumonia and catarrh. Even today, a person with a badly infected chest will be encouraged to 'get up the phlegm', and modern pharmaceutical cold cures are advertised as capable of 'loosening' phlegm and bringing relief to 'tight' chests. Though originally phlegm was seen as a causal agency in the body related to cold wet constrictions, it was to become specifically identified with nasal and respiratory mucus. That this mucus could somehow invade the lungs and throat still produces graphic images of an evil substance clogging up one's passages, and figures prominently in many of the descriptions of chest diseases related to me by elderly people.

The basis of most traditional chest cures which I encountered hinged on the power of the remedy to 'cut the phlegm'[8] and prize it loose, so that the sufferer could cough it up. The image conjured up for such cures was of a respiratory solvent which quarried the phlegm and eroded it away. References to 'cutting and purging' phlegm out of the vital passages are legion, and tell us much about how the internal processes of the body were imagined.

All of the humours were thought to be responsive to heat, and blood, bile and phlegm could be coaxed around the body by its judicious application. Heat, after all, was a pivotal property in nature in general, as well as in medicine in particular, lying at the heart of growth and seasonal change. The simplest test to separate the quick from the dead was to see if any heat still resided in the body, while ageing itself was conceived as a progressive cooling process culminating in death. The English obsession with draughts, damp and keeping dry formed part of the same syndrome, no doubt intensified by conditions of climate. It was better to be warm and dry than it was to be clean, and the foetid snugness of many homes must have provided ideal conditions for the transmission of many infections.

An essential part of popular heat therapeutics lay in 'drawing' a disorder or imbalance. Placing one's feet in a tub of hot water could help the sufferer with a bad cold by helping to draw the blood and other thick obstructions away from the head. Drawing inevitably worked by moving things in contrary directions to restore a balance, though the inadvertent application of a drawing agent could also upset a natural process. One Salford lady related in considerable detail how her mother had argued that if a menstruating woman washed her hair, the hot water would attract the blood upwards to the brain, rather than downwards, as should have been its natural direction at such a time.[9]

Hot applications to the chest were ascribed an almost universal efficacy, especially for the young. 'Thermogene' was a popular patent lint fabric, pieces of which were fastened to the chests and backs of 'delicate' children and left *in situ* all winter through.[10] I was told of one person whose childhood in the 1920s saw many ailments, and who wore 'Thermogene' for months on end. The pad would be picked away by his mother to progressively reduce it in size as winter gave way to spring, to let the fresh air get at his chest. Chest poultices were made of a variety of substances, many of them more traditional than 'Thermogene'. A sheet of brown paper would be thickly caked with candle tallow or dripping and tied around the chest or back, with the grease next to the skin. The poultice became even more efficacious if the paper had received numerous pin-pricks prior to application to enable it to 'breathe'.[11] A Pendlebury pigeon fancier, in an incident dating from around 1921, saved the life of his pneumonia-stricken young son by the application of a pigeon to the child's chest as the illness reached its crisis. Though the application of living creatures to the body to provide a drawing heat is of immemorial ancestry, the pigeon in question seems to have been killed and partially dismembered beforehand, for as my informant related, 'he was covered in blood in the morning, but the pneumonia had gone'. How many layers of folk belief in sympathetic magic were being invoked here is a matter for speculation; an animal life to save a human, the smearing of the sick with sacrificial blood in the hope of stimulating the patient's own life blood to overcome the sickness?[12]

Hot 'rubs' and embrocations, especially to the chest, were also seen as ways of providing a drawing heat. Because of the tingling effect which certain astringent substances have upon the skin, there has long been the belief that particular plants and chemicals possess an innate heat. Classical pharmacy and *materia medica* had used the principle extensively, and the basis of allopathic medicine had resided in administering substances which would provoke symptoms contrary to those of the disease. This belief was quite probably aided by the fact that an injured part often feels better when kept warm and that sprained or injured muscles relax under heat. The proprietary 'mentholated' embrocation

Deep Heat, which is still sold, also evokes in the mind of the sufferer the presence of a benign warming agent, sinking deep into the joint.

Yet how a chest poultice or embrocation was expected to work on the lungs or trachea is less obvious. I have asked several elderly respondents how goose grease, tallow or the popular rub 'Vick' were expected to penetrate several inches of bone, fat and muscle to get at the lungs and act on the phlegm, and have invariably received quasi-magical responses. The chest poultice or embrocation worked mysteriously, as its innate heat drove out the cold malignancy from the lungs. An alternative explanation suggested that the pungent spirituous aroma of chest rubs such as 'Vick' were breathed by the child as he or she became warm, and acted on the lungs by inhalation.

One of the most conspicuously successful ways in which the centrality of heat in classical Greek medicine was married-up with Victorian theories of power and energy, however, was in the teachings of the Americans, Dr J.A. Coffin and Dr Thomson, and their disciples. Their ideas came to be extremely influential in English fringe medicine around 1846, when Dr Coffin settled in Manchester. Dr Thomson's 'system', which was said to coincide with Coffin's, was a form of steam engine physiology, in which the heart was a boiler, liquids moved under pressure, and food was equivalent to coal and produced a 'vital principle' which was the same as mechanical energy. Heat, therefore was primary, and imbalances in this vital force lay at the root of all disease, for they upset the healthy equipoise of the four elements. These imbalances could be rectified by the application of such herbs as lobelia and cayenne pepper and one or two others, administered in special doses. An account of the 'Coffinite' system was produced by William Fox under the socially specific title of *The Working Man's Model Family Botanic Guide, or Every Man His Own Doctor*; while a 'Coffinite' dispensary was still said to have been operating in the Oldham district of greater Manchester as late as World War II.[13]

There were magical aspects of disease that were not only based on a belief in vital forces and the power of opposites, but also on astrology. Though not connected with the modern cult of astrology, many of my respondents held firm, if vague, convictions that the heavens bore some relation to a person's state of health. The apparent connection between the heavens and the processes of life is, after all, an obvious one, and even as early as 1748, Dr Richard Mead – an academic physician of eminence and a disciple of Sir Isaac Newton – tried to explain some correlations in purely physical terms.[14] As the Sun and Moon moved around the sky, argued Mead, their gravitational forces changed, thereby producing long- and short-term cycles, to which the human body was most likely sensitive. Explanations along contemporary lines have been put forward by such writers as Lyell Watson.[15] With such a lineage, it is hardly surprising that celestial causes of disease figure so prominently in folk medicine.

The celestial body most commonly ascribed medical properties was the Moon. Perhaps because of its prominence and ever-changing shape, not to mention its 28-day cycle, it became the cause of the 'Moon's disease' in women from at least classical times down to the twentieth century. *Aristotle's Works* in its Victorian editions was quite unequivocal in this ascription, and must have continued to give written substantiation to an ancient folk belief. The correlation between the lunar and reproductive cycles is of course far from resolved even today.[16]

The Moon was also believed to influence the minds of both sexes, though for obvious reasons women were generally held to be more susceptible than men. The classical explanation for hysteria – from the Greek word for the womb, *hystera* – lay in the belief that the womb could rise up and move around the woman's body. Its wanderings were often triggered by lunar influences, which could result in its placing pressure on other organs, thereby producing 'hysterical' behaviour.[17] The shape of the full Moon also gave substance to the ideas of 'Moon-faced' individuals, as well as large 'harvest Moon' backsides. The Moon also affected the state of mind, and lunacy was traditionally attributed to it. The 'loony' on the one hand and the 'mooning' lover on the other represent the graphic residues of this once vivid imagery. For centuries, the word 'mooncalf' was applied to the mentally retarded or wild, and the primitive Caliban in Shakespeare's *The Tempest* was given that description.[18] My grandmother firmly believed that people could be 'moonstruck' and when as a boy, I became interested in astronomy, she considered that looking at our satellite through a home-made telescope was potentially a dangerous hobby.

In addition to a possible lunar connection, madness and mental trouble were often ascribed to general weaknesses of the person. Perhaps the embarrassment which still surrounds so much family discussion of nervous and mental disorders today owes something to the belief that persons afflicted by them were either endemically weak, or else attention-seekers. To a race of people so stoical and emotionally restrained as the Edwardian working class, the kind of emotional exhibition which mental illness often involved must have seemed profoundly shocking. 'Loonies', like illegitimate children, cast a major blight on the respectable pedigree of any working-class family. Though respondents who spoke of these matters with me no longer regarded the mentally upset as social pariahs, their own recollections back to parental and grandparental attitudes at the turn of the century confirm the survival of the ancient belief.

My grandfather, who was a man of the greatest natural gentleness, was convinced that most mentally disturbed people simply 'could not get a proper grip over themselves', or else were seeking publicity. 'There is no cure for 'nerves', only self-control and will-power', he would say. Madness, like fever, was an ever-lurking predator, or demon, ready to pull down those who lacked the power to resist it. He told the story of a Pendlebury woman of *circa* 1914, who was prone to hysterical fits and shrieking. This scenario usually won her a great deal of attention from neighbours, until her husband started throwing buckets of cold water over her every time she had a fit. Grandfather's belief in the self-display and self-healing character of mental disorders was confirmed when the woman suddenly stopped having her attacks. As an attitude towards the mentally sick, however, it would not have been too far removed from that of Victorian physicians who believed in electric shock treatments, or even their eighteenth-century counterparts who tried to physically restrain the deranged George III.[19] Though done for different reasons, one must not forget that cerebral shock treatment was also available on the National Health, and as boy I remember the hushed and embarrassed tone in which my grandmother and aunts discussed the state of a distant relative who was subjected to it around 1958.

Bad airs and stinks were thought to be the agents whereby infectious diseases were transmitted. The fevers which came in summer were held to be the products of unemptied ash-pit middens, butcher's offal and the like. My grandmother firmly believed in a correlation between bad smells and infectious diseases, in the same way as she believed that other sorts of smells such as those produced by burning tar or sulphur were wholesome, and cleansed the air. This concern with smells no doubt received some substantiation in her case from conversations with her own grandmother, Mrs Martha Halliday, who remembered the plague (or cholera) epidemics which had ravaged the industrial districts of Manchester during her childhood in the middle years of the nineteenth century. This was probably the great epidemic of 1848. Mrs Halliday remembered the collection of the dead on public waggons (usually at night) and the communal burial pits, or so her granddaughter related one hundred and twenty years later. My grandfather, who possessed an excellent memory, combined with a compelling way of telling old and grisly tales, used to relate that when a railway cutting was being dug in Swinton, some years before he was born in 1891, the workmen accidentally broke open a cholera pit. The lime-soaked dead who had been interred in it were so well preserved as to still be recognisable, while the effluvias that rose up out of the pit were said to have killed the workmen who breathed them.

The explanation of diseases in terms of stinks and 'miasmas' was as perfect a piece of classical pathology as one could wish for. Hippocrates had attributed fevers to them, as did many subsequent medical writers.[20] Indeed, the poisonous nature of bad smells was one of the last pieces of classical pathology to be formally discarded by academic medicine, for not until Pasteur expounded his germ theory in the 1860s was an adequate alternative suggested. Though my grandmother, in the years that I knew her, spoke of germs, she seemed to hold them hand in glove with a more established belief in the poisonous nature of stinks, as did many of her contemporaries with whom I have spoken.

The conventions of language in which people speak of disease also tells us much about how the disease is imagined. One senses that certain words were and are to be avoided when discussing medical problems, as though their use constituted either a confession or an invitation to fate. One elderly member of my family, for instance, never used such words as 'sickness' or 'illness' when describing disease. Instead, everything would either be 'bad' or, *in extremis*, 'rotten'. Whether the ailing person of whom he spoke had a terminal illness or nothing more than a severe cold, they were all uniformly 'bad'. Several medical practitioners who have supplied me with material relating to the way in which patients described their complaints in the consulting room concurred on this partiality for blanket euphemisms. It must have demanded great patience and diagnostic skill in a physician to form an accurate assessment of a patient who could only make embarrassed grunts about his 'back, belly and two sides'.

I suspect that the reluctance to openly describe or discuss particular diseases, even when unconnected with sexual complaints, derives from two sources. One of these is a silent stoicism; the other, a superstitious dread of inadvertently invoking that which is most feared. Disease names could, after all, be like magic words. That virtue of stiff-upper-lip stoicism which is often thought to be peculiarly English persists with especial tenacity in the older working class; it may be part and parcel of that necessary toughness found in the successful survivors in a struggle for life, or the belief that to admit to being ill was a sign of weakness in a proud person. Either way, it was prized equally by both men and women. Though every sympathy was extended to the genuinely sick, there was a derisory contempt for those soft or 'marred' people who cried too easily or showed their feelings. Admiration went to those who could 'suffer in silence', while a hushed respect was extended to those who were known to bear a heavy burden. Certain persons were 'martyrs' to their back, digestion, bowels or liver, while the popular 1930s comedian Sandy Powell successfully sent up the perpetual medical moaner with the catch phrase 'Oh, the agony, Ivy' in his sketches.

The word 'cancer' is still often spoken in soft tones, after euphemism has failed, as if careful not to irritate a sleeping demon. People once spoke of TB in the same way. Perhaps because cancer is one of the last great killers, people often concentrate many of their medical fears upon this disease in a way which would have been less acute in an age when tuberculosis, diabetes and many other maladies were also incurable and commonplace. Yet the very derivation of the word itself shows how people have visualised it over the centuries. Coming from the Latin word for crab (and still enshrined in the zodiacal sign), it was, and is, seen as something furtive, creeping and sharp, forever expanding, with claws ready to grasp and constrict the organs. Just as pulmonary consumption was popularly visualised as the lungs clogging up, so cancer was a viciously greedy predator. Its almost independent, self-determining power of action is summed up in the idea that people are 'got' by cancer, in the same way as the unfortunate traveller was 'got' by wolves in the forest. Because of the way in which terminal cancer often emaciates the body, moreover, it is easy to imagine the growth, almost of its own conscious volition, actively consuming its victim. When Mrs Morel is dying of cancer in D.H. Lawrence's *Sons and Lovers*, her two children try to slowly starve her in spite of her appetite, in the hope that by failing to feed the growth, which itself ate up all the food they gave her, they might effect a merciful release.[21] Many people have also voiced to me the belief that cancer could be caught or contracted from the persons or clothing of existing sufferers. The established status of this folk belief is demonstrated by the fate of Mr Crass, the odious, light-fingered chargehand in Tressell's *The Ragged Trousered*

Philanthropists, who purloined a wrap from the house of a lady who had died from cancer, only to develop a growth on his own face :

'He always wore the warm wrap that had belonged to the old lady who died of cancer. However, Crass did not worry about this little sore place; he just put a little zinc ointment on it occasionally and had no doubt that it would get well in time'.[22]

Another set of folk beliefs which indicates a popular pathology relates to diseases and conditions of the heart. Because the heart, in both classical and later physiology, was seen as central to the maintenance of life, any impediment to its functions was seen as dangerous. Before William Harvey discovered, in 1628, that the heart was really a pump which propelled the blood around the body, the organ was believed to be the place where 'life' was blown into the blood from the lungs, and hence was the centre of all heat and vital processes. As the very centre of life, it also controlled emotion, and if it came to be 'broken', life would cease. A languishing death, following great disappointment or sadness, came when this emotionally sensitive organ could take no more. As pointed out earlier, we still use this ancient physiology when people talk about their feelings, and it is still through the heart that Cupid shoots his arrows on St Valentine's Day cards. Cowards, moreover, are not only traditionally 'weak-hearted', but have been known to possess the hearts of timorous animals. Who has not heard of those despised wretches who possess the hearts of lambs, rabbits or chickens, or the hero who possessed the heart of a lion? Classical physiology generally agreed that one could imbibe the strength of brave creatures by eating their hearts and sometimes drinking the blood which passed through them. Bull's hearts were prized in this respect, while one lady told me of her younger brother in the 1930s who requested his mother to get him some 'pluck' from the butcher's to give him the courage and strength to overcome school bullies. 'Pluck' was an animal entrail often fed to dogs and cats, which was thought to strengthen their

Monsterous births' or deformities. These woodcut characters illustrating deformities were standard inclusions in *The Works of Aristotle*, being copied line for line from the early nineteenth and into the twentieth centuries. *The Works of Aristotle the Famous Philosopher* (Moritz & Chambers, London, *c.*1910–20), pp.39–40. Though undated, this edition of Aristotle, with its two-tone colour-plates, must date from the early twentieth century. (Author's collection.)

hearts to make them fighters; and one can only assume that such specimens of folk magic, if they were requested by schoolboys, were well known to the people at large.

Alongside the emotional role of the heart, folk medicine by the nineteenth century was willing to attribute to it a parallel function which acknowledged its status as a pump. This is best seen in the various references to 'fatty' hearts which I have encountered, both in verbal recollections from elderly people, and also from literature. Fatty hearts were believed to be endangered by a ring of fat which grew insidiously around the organ, and which on becoming complete, strangled it and extinguished life. My maternal great-grandfather, John Platt, who died in 1908, had allegedly been told beforehand by his doctor that this was his fate, and that the fat was building up into a ring, not unlike an over-tight collar. My grandfather, who related this account from his youth, stated that his father

Aristotle, complete with all the theatrical trappings of the Renaissance wise physician – hourglass, globes, stuffed animals, and skeleton – demonstrating the mysteries of womanhood. *The Works of Aristotle the Famous Philosopher* (Moritz & Chambers, London, *c.*1910–20), frontispiece. (Author's collection.)

died when the ring became complete. This clearly parallels the death of the fictional Durbeyfield, father of Hardy's *Tess of the D'Urbervilles* (1891), who also died from a strangulating ring of fat around his heart.[23] Though I have not found this explanation being used to account for contemporary heart

'Medical Knowledge': ancient wisdom on babies and their care. *The Works of Aristotle the Famous Philosopher* (Moritz & Chambers, London, *c.*1910–20), third frontispiece. (Author's collection.)

deaths, it does have an interesting latter-day variant in the parental admonition against the use of chewing gum, as related by one of my informants. This gentleman, who grew up in the 1930s, was told by his mother that if he swallowed the gum, it would wrap itself around his heart and kill him![24]

Although there were many avenues through which this antique physiology was perpetuated in folk medicine, one of

Classical Cherubic Healers minister to a Greek soldier, emphasising the classical wisdom supposedly implicit in *Aristotle's Works*. *The Works of Aristotle the Famous Philosopher* (Moritz & Chambers, London, *c*.1910–20), second frontispiece. (Author's collection.)

them must have been the ubiquitous *Aristotle's Works*. The copies which I have examined relate extensive information about how the body was believed to function, both in sickness and in health, the greater part of which was entirely obsolete by the time of publication in the days of Queen Victoria.

The central section of *Aristotle's Works,* known as 'Aristotle's Masterpiece', dealt with the physiology of reproduction. Conception was spoken of as being similar to gardening, in which the woman represented the dormant principle – the earth – while the man was the active seed. When the 'seeds' of both sexes were combined in copulation, the 'heat' involved was seen as triggering vital processes which would commence the foetus. The man was seen as contributing the catalysing agent, so that the dormant potential of the woman moved towards the actualisation of the child.[25] Conception itself was seen as a curdling process caused by the presence of the male 'seed' in the blood contained in the womb. In a woman who was not pregnant, this blood was lost by menstruation, though after conception it was retained to nourish the foetus, while some of it was transformed into breast milk, and stored for later use. Blood, in short, was the quintessential substance of life.

Many features of classical Greek medicine lie at the heart of this explanation in *Aristotle's Works*: the obvious primacy of blood, the male–female, active–passive roles, and the belief that life formed out of a curdling together at one end of the scale, in the same way as death was a dissolution at the other.

The 1857 edition of *Aristotle's Works* discusses the anatomy of the womb, and the two chambers in which it was believed children were conceived. Though 'Aristotle's Masterpiece' argued that male children were conceived in the right-hand chamber (from the warmth of the nearby liver, which engendered blood), and females in the left (from the coldness of the spleen), the passage also discusses the contrary opinion of Hippocrates, who was an even earlier Greek physician.[26] Nowhere does one encounter any remotely modern information, and none at all from the nineteenth century.

Aristotle's Works also discusses the assumed causes of barrenness. Using the classical doctrine of 'complexions' and 'temperaments', it is stated that sterility often results when two persons of the same type attempt to mate:

> 'For the universal course of nature being formed of contraries, [it] cannot be increased by the composition of likes; therefore, if the constitution of the woman be hot and dry [choleric], as well as the man's, there can be no conception.'[27]

Similarly, sterility would result if two persons of cold, moist (phlegmatic) temperament also tried to reproduce. Conception thus best occurred when the two parties were different in complexion, such as a 'hot' woman and a 'cold' man, so that their opposite natures would produce something fresh, rather than something like themselves.

None of these explanations would have possessed any serious scientific credibility by the second half of the nineteenth century, and quite apart from the classical Greek theories about hot and cold natures and the curdling of blood, the book was also full of straightforward anatomical mistakes. The human womb, for instance, does not have the two 'horns' – attributed to it by the ancient anatomists – in which it generates male and female children, nor does the liver produce the blood or the heart act as a kettle in which it is boiled.

Elsewhere in *Aristotle's Works,* questions and answers are set, dealing with popular medical topics, all of which are discussed in the conceptual language of the ancient Greeks rather than that of nineteenth-century physiology. We are told, for instance, that a disordered stomach makes one feel unwell because the stomach is 'knit with the brain, heart and liver' and upsets their balance.[28] The 'gall' was believed to be connected with the spleen, thereby creating hot choleric dispositions and bad tempers, while mild-natured animals, such as sheep and pigeons, derived their passivity from a lack of this humour.[29] In the section entitled 'Aristotle's Problems', which purported to answer all sorts of questions in medicine and physiology, the mode of explanation is straightforwardly humoral. It clearly states that there are four humours, that these cause the main 'temperaments', and that heat, cold, and the like lie at the heart of all things.

Another essential ingredient in this style of explanation is the ancient idea that rising and falling, in and out, and ebb and flow also constitute primary physiological processes. One is told, for instance, that men feel tired after hard labour because heat naturally travels from the inner parts outwards. Upon resting, however, the heat 'digests' in the internal parts (as sweating ceases), and thereby turns into vapours which rise from the heart to the brain. Yet because the brain is cold, these hot spirits cool, thicken and fail to disperse, and from their sluggishness sleep is produced.[30] In sleep, different types of dreams originate from different humours or temperaments: merry dreams come from Blood, frightening dreams from Black Bile, violent dreams from Yellow Bile, and watery dreams from Phlegm.[31]

Many of the explanations and procedures of the physiology of the people can be related in some way to *Aristotle's Works*, for in its popular Victorian editions it had ceased to be just a book for midwives and mothers, and became a general *vade mecum* of medicine and natural history. I can find echoes of many of my grandfather's remarks about plants and animals in its pages, along with folk medicine's overall preoccupation with heat, blood and humours. It is not my argument that *Aristotle's Works* provided the basic grounding for the medical tradition outlined in this book, but that it lent substantiation and written proof to those literate persons wishing to read up specific points. The Medicine of the People comes through many diverse, mainly oral channels, though the persistent popularity of a Victorian publication which reiterated ancient Greek notions about the body cannot be underestimated. While my informants on the whole did not wish to go into detail regarding this 'embarrassing' publication, I found many people who were nonetheless familiar with it. Whilst most of my informants, moreover, would have been too young to have ranked amongst the mainstream Victorian readers of 'Aristotle', its persistent presence in the 'little bottom drawers' of many early twentieth-century working-class households is substantiated by Gracie Fields.[32]

In the last two decades of the nineteenth century, many people became alarmed at the general medical ignorance of the working classes, especially pertaining to sexual matters, and their tendency to over-breed. In consequence, a number of cheap and simple publications began to appear to provide more accurate and up-to-date information than could be found in 'Aristotle'.

The dual purpose of imparting useful information and hoping to arrest the rising lower-class birth rate produced some interesting publications which aimed to extend the precepts of 'Malthusianism', or birth control, from the middle to the working classes. These pamphlets were invariably short, being between a dozen and fifty pages in length, and costing no more than a few coppers. The *Words of Wisdom on Courtship and Marriage* by W. George (undated, *circa* 1890) makes its message clear from the start with a pair of pictures in the frontispiece.[33] Two families are depicted: one consists of a well-dressed middle-class couple with two children, while the other shows a slum hovel, with six starving offspring. Birth control is the way to prosperity, and the pamphlet goes on to describe the basic functions of reproduction, and how it can be prevented by the proprietary syringes, enemas, sheaths and pessaries advertised on the book's inside covers. John M. Robertson's *Over-Population: a Lecture* (1890) fulfils a similar mission.[34]

It was Dr H.A. Allbutt who set himself up as the most tireless educator of the poor on matters of birth control, reproduction and child care. It was his aim to provide a simple book

'which could be understood by most women and at a price which would ensure it a place even in the poorest household'.[35]

Allbutt's *Wife's Handbook* (1886) discusses half a dozen different birth control methods, chemical and mechanical, all of which work in varying degrees. His other pamphlet publications, usually costing around sixpence per copy, dealt with such subjects as child care, the reduction of infant mortality, and sexual hygiene.[36]

In spite of the good intentions of these publications, they were but drops in the ocean alongside the weight of popular medical tradition. The very fact that most of these self-styled educators were committed birth control advocates probably damned them outright in the eyes of most working-class people, who tended to regard such practices as immoral and unnatural.   Indeed, one might argue that they were counterproductive, associating 'modern physiology' in the popular mind with 'dirty books', and thereby reinforcing the traditional precepts which said that nature must be left to take its course, and not be talked about.

Although possessing no consciously articulated physiology or pathology, the traditional Medicine of the People nonetheless contained a clear set of assumptions about how the body was believed to work and how disease was produced. Listening to many elderly people talking about their own medical ideas, or those recalled from their parents, one finds rules of health rooted in balance and the action of vital and malignant forces. One finds a collection of notions where words possess some sort of power, and nature forms a divine unity linking the heavens with the Earth to comprise a quasi-moral system in which the 'good' of life must be strengthened against the 'bad' of death. Good things rise and poisons fall, heat radiates outwards whereas cold festers within, while the whole is bound together in the ever-changing relationships of blood, bile and phlegm.

While I have encountered no living person who believes in or consciously acts upon this system in its entirety, its components have emerged as folk-fragments in the same conversations with respondents familiar with heart transplants and antibiotics. The current generation of elderly people are, needless to say, very much better informed and educated than were their own parents, and have picked up their modern ideas from television, radio, magazines and fifty years of socialised medicine. Yet in spite of this awareness, it is truly remarkable how much of the ancestral tradition still remains if one but cares to look for it.

4

Popular remedies and procedures

At the very heart of the Medicine of the People lay the remedies themselves. Vague and nonsensical as these procedures may often appear to us, they remained rooted in an overall approach to disease outlined in the previous chapters, and contained a sound logic of their own. The supposed efficacy of a mode of treatment or preventive action generally lay in the way by which it would restore a balance to the body, unblock something stopped up, or impart heat to that which was cold. Remedies were often valued for their immemorial antiquity or 'naturalness', working on the assumption that if a thing had been in use for as long as anyone could remember, then it must work, combined with the belief that nature's way is always the best. In this respect, Victorian folk medicine remained close to the precepts of classical and Renaissance medicine, with its axiomatic conservatism and underlying assumption that if a thing was truly beneficial, then God would not have permitted it to remain concealed for hundreds of years. The 'good old cures' were therefore the best.

The 'natural' character of a medicine was also important. To qualify thus, a medicine had first to be old, and then compounded out of simple materials, preferably herbal in origin. The persistent belief in the naturalness of herbs has enjoyed a remarkable comeback in modern alternative medicine, with its stress on the layman's ability to take charge of his or her health, coupled with the popular image of the wholesomeness of fields and meadows. This way of viewing sickness and health is also firmly anchored in an essentially simplistic way of looking at disease. It is a world innocent of bacteria, physiological malfunctions, genetics and biochemistry; a world unacquainted with, or else which prefers to ignore, the extraordinary complexity of the human body and the wide variety of ways in which it can go wrong. Natural medicine sees clear and simple alternatives: healthy or diseased, wholesome or poisoned, good or bad. It is still a world in which illness carries moral overtones, and where the cures are 'virtuous' and the diseases 'nasty'. It is still the world of our great-grandparents, of Wesley and Hippocrates.

The innate simplicity of approach in folk medicine, be it Victorian or contemporary, further stems from a deeply held mistrust of experts. The professional physician, with his arcane training and incomprehensible words, is seen as possessing a power which the ordinary person cannot really trust. Self-medication lies at the centre of folk medicine, and forms a consistent theme in the discussions and letters which I have had and exchanged with people while researching the present study. If you 'got yourself right', it combined the virtues of economy with a deliverance from the machinations of experts, although this persistent tendency often meant that even long after the National Health Service had been founded, a reliance on placebos and stoical long-suffering left many treatable diseases to run to a fatal termination.

The most popular self-therapeutic procedure was the purge. Human bodies, like houses and hen coops, needed a regular spring clean, for it was thought that nasty humours came to settle in the body if they were not regularly removed. When one considers the dietary conditions of the Victorian working class, however, the popular logic made more sense than it would today. In an age without effective food preservation – at least for the poor – the body would have become progressively undernourished during the winter months. The appearance of boils, inflammations and bronchial coughs towards the end of winter would constitute characteristic symptoms, as the absence of fresh fruit and vegetables took their toll. One old lady told me how the poisons built up in the body, and the blood became clogged up with 'waste matter', to cause boils and skin eruptions. A good purge was then needed to set things right, expel the poisons, purify the blood, and get rid of the 'matter'.[1]

Many people with whom I spoke used the image of a hibernation falling upon the body's organs during the winter, causing their functions to become sluggish and waste products to accumulate. The process of release was best performed by brimstone (sulphur) and black treacle, which in itself continued a tradition of centuries. Venice Treacle and other treacle preparations had been standbys in Renaissance pharmacy, when purging was still a major therapeutic device of academic medicine. Brimstone and treacle, moreover, was the favourite 'physicking' administered by Mrs Squeers 'to purify the boys' blood now and then' to the unfortunate inmates of Dotheboy's Hall in Dickens' *Nicholas Nickleby*, where it also possessed the financially convenient property of being an appetite suppressant.[2] The popularity of treacle purges in the late nineteenth century was confirmed by many people, including John Evans, who as Britain's oldest man discussed the matter in a BBC2 television documentary interview which he gave on the eve of his one hundred and ninth birthday, in 1986.[3]

Sulphur enjoyed a pre-eminent place as a cleansing agent, and was frequently added to purging mixtures. Perhaps this popularity related to sulphur's long-standing use as a disinfectant; when burned it could kill 'bugs', the traditional name for cockroaches, in an enclosed room, while during medieval and early modern plague epidemics, contaminated letters and fabrics were 'cleansed' by passing them through burning sulphur fumes.[4]

Purges, one must remember, did not just apply to the alimentary canal, but could be used to shift obstructions from wherever anything needed to be unblocked in the body. Spirits of Hartshorn (ammonia, or 'armonia' as it was commonly pronounced) could purge the nose and brain in cases of chronic catarrh, while the universally popular sulphur could be rubbed into boils and rashes to purge the skin, and be eaten raw to purge the blood. My grandmother believed that sulphur had a cooling action on the blood (a fragment of ancient pharmacy in itself), and that its prescription to young or adolescent persons in spring time cooled that overheated blood which caused skin rashes and acne. As a teenager, about 1960, I was often prescribed 'flowers of sulphur' by my grandmother, both as a skin rub and taken internally, for spots and rashes, where it was supposed to purge the hot dregs from the blood. At every stage, however, the image of the malady was that of a blockage to a vital process which had to be unbunged to permit accumulated poisons to escape and nature's balance to be restored.

Many medical persons who have supplied me with material have emphasised the great significance attributed to 'open bowels' in vernacular medicine, and how their professional services were eventually called upon by patients *in extremis* for whom black treacle, syrup of figs and rhubarb had failed. One doctor, who had first practised in the Bolton area in the late 1930s, told me that severe constipation was one of the commonest 'simple' maladies about which working people went to see the doctor before the days of the National Health Service. He told me that the condition was usually diagnosed by the expression on the patient's face even before they spoke. The embarrassed patient would sit down and search for words, before exclaiming 'Doctor, I have na bin for over a week.'[5]

Self-administered purges were spoken of with warm approbation, usually equating them with explosives or mighty solvents, which tells us immediately how people visualised their illnesses. There was nothing like a real good purge that would 'shift the rock of Gibraltar'.

They were like gunpowder or dynamite, and one elderly Welsh collier graphically equated his favourite patent purge with a shot cartridge used in the mines to blast the coal loose. One wonders whether its importance as an ingredient in gunpowder had anything to do with the inclusion of sulphur in many purges.[6]

Sulphur was also used as a 'tonic', while one should remember that tonics in themselves formed a popular and almost universal class of medicines. As a purge cleansed, so a tonic fortified and strengthened. Though tonics were given to the convalescent, they were also taken as health preservatives by the well. The 'Laxy Vitrall' (Elixir of Vitriol?), by which Mr Morel swore in Lawrence's *Sons and Lovers*, was one of a myriad of patent tonics and purges on sale in the early twentieth century, and as Lawrence stated, colliers and working people spent on them lavishly. In the same novel, Lawrence spoke of Morel's fondness for his own health preparation, which he brewed up over the fire from herbs and simples.[7]

Alcohol was also a favourite ingredient of many tonics, and 'tonic wines' formed a popular line for those persons who felt that by drinking these medicinal preparations, one received invigoration without the taint of the demon drink. The frequency with which alcohol was added to patent tonics and such preparations was disclosed by the British Medical Association in its analytical exposé, *Secret Remedies*, in 1908.[8] In the late nineteenth century, 'Cocoa Wines' had been marketed for their tonic value, at a time when the newly-discovered cocaine, a South American plant extract, was thought to lift the spirits without the risk of addiction which accompanied alcohol.[9]

Tonics, like purges, remained true to the practice of vernacular medicine insofar as they saw health as a balance which needed to be restored and cleansed. They touched upon the 'vital' processes of nature in some mysterious way, rather than relating to scientific cause and effect. By their easy operation, both in theory and practice, they were familiar to all, and not the preserve of a professional élite, thereby fitting into a view of health which proclaimed that self-medication was best.

Cures, in their various forms, were usually most prized for their power of invoking symptoms or images contrary from those of the diseases, as in the case of giving something warm to reverse a cold disease. The treatment of coughs clearly bore out this way of thinking. As coughs and respiratory disorders were generally envisaged as being caused by cold phlegm adhering to the lungs and throat, so the best way to dissolve or cut it was by a thick, warm substance. Cough medicines, by definition, had to be viscous. My grandfather's test for such a medicine was something so thick and warm that you could feel it 'slithering slowly down your throat', and where it was necessary to strike the upturned bottle with the flat of the hand before the glutinous contents would even move. The psychological imagery of such medicines was powerful, and was also pointed out by Robert Roberts. When talking about the commodities sold in his mother's corner shop in Edwardian Salford, Roberts told of a local patent medicines manufacturer who brought a cough cure onto the market, but which was not selling well. It was suggested that it was too thin and watery for such a medicine, and that he should add something to make it thicker. Following this advice, he added an emulsifying agent to the mixture, thereby transforming his compound into a profitable line.[10]

Many of the persons who gave me information about respiratory or throat ailments used the phrase that the medicine should 'cut the phlegm'. In this way, the lungs and vocal chords were cleansed, and the patient was able to cough it up. Bronchial specifics were, indeed, seen as a form of purge, as the medicine was imagined as dissolving, cutting or breaking up the phlegm so that it could come up. One still encounters the Lancashire phrase uttered to someone with a constricted throat: 'Cough it up, it might be a piano.'

Of all the medicines in popular use, it is probably true to say that purges and cough specifics were the most widespread. Home-made specifics usually had a clear herbal base – liquorice and buckthorn being favourites – to which easily obtainable pharmaceutical preparations could be added. Chlorodyne, a late nineteenth-century proprietary analgesic, was sometimes added, and probably substituted for the opium (chlorodyne contains morphine) used in earlier recipes.[11] A successful cough medicine needed two ingredients: something to create a sensation of warm viscosity, and a sedative. Quite often the really active ingredient was the chlorodyne or opiate, which suppressed the cough reflex when the drug entered the brain via the bloodstream, thereby enabling the person to sleep. In the cold damp of a north-country winter, one of the worst aspects of a cough was its power to prevent sleep, which the opiate would overcome. Though many of the herbal ingredients in these medicines would have contributed the odd vitamin, their real power lay in the action of the analgesic. The opiate or alcohol, depending upon what proportions were present, would lift the spirits and make one sleep. The addition of purgatives to cough mixtures may well have been intended to counteract the costiveness which an opiate would otherwise have produced, though one Pendlebury chemist, Teddy Banks, was the retailer of a popular specific which was also prized for its purgative action. It seems to have worked as a cough suppressant by a curious route, according to the gentleman who related the account to me: 'One good swig, and you daren't cough for the rest o' the day. When your throat tickled in t' street, you had to hold your breath.'[12]

Until quite recently, it was possible to find pharmaceutical chemists in the north (and probably elsewhere) who would 'make up' a cough bottle in accordance with the intended purchaser's favourite ingredients. The measured ingredients would be placed in a bottle of standard volume, and could be taken away either neat, or with water added. My father said that it was common to hear coal-miner customers in a Pendlebury chemist's shop asking for their medicines neat, saying 'I can stick it under my own tap at home.' This may have derived from the belief that chemists charged for the water which they added to a preparation.

Greases and oils were also believed to possess an innate power of healing, and Elizabeth Roberts has suggested that this may possibly derive from the ancient use of oil as a sacred ointment.[13] Mention has already been made of the hot 'rubs', which were usually of an oily character, though oils and greases figured in more mysterious ways. My grandmother employed oils (of which olive was her favourite) to anoint the temples and foreheads of the sick. Babies especially were thought to derive great benefit from this procedure, and it could be administered for teething convulsions, and a wide range of disorders. This almost sacerdotal act, with its roots in pre-Reformation times, would have horrified my Wesleyan grandmother had it been suggested to her that it might in some way have been related to 'priestcraft' and Roman Catholicism.

Similarly, salt fulfilled a wide variety of purposes as a cleansing agent. When rubbed into wounds, it was believed to both ward off infection and improve the blood. Salt was also exposed in the presence of dead bodies, being laid out in the house prior to burial. As a girl, my grandmother recalled heaped plates of salt being placed on the chest of corpses, supposedly 'to stop them from bursting' . One wonders how this came down as a Protestant version of the ancient practice of sin-eating, where the sins of the dead were absorbed into a dish of salt, to be consumed by the living in a funeral meal, thereby lightening the soul of the departed – redolent, indeed, of the Roman Catholic doctrine of Purgatory.[14] This could well have given rise to the working-class practice of treating the mourners, after a funeral, to a tea of salted ham – 'buried with 'am', as it was called.

Many folk cures display a surprising resilience and capacity to adapt to changing ideas, both in medicine and life in general. One could still purchase, in 1986, a viscous proprietary rub called Dog Oil, manufactured and sold by a small firm in Lancashire. Quite probably this white, odourless and almost translucent grease possessed an ancestry going back to the 'bear fat' and 'goose grease' of earlier practice, where it was popularly believed that creatures possessing warm coats – be they of fur, feathers, or hair – were less prone to rheumatism and stiffness. The present proprietary Dog Oil, however, catering no doubt for a world more inclined to vegetarianism and animal-friendly products, now boasts on its label to contain neither drugs nor animal substances. Precisely what the present drugless, vegetable substance possesses which is supposed to be medically efficacious, and what connection it has with dogs, is not clear. What it does show is the ingenious way in which an old remedy can be changed to suit the tastes of new users. Perhaps its continued success derives from the comfort which most joints receive when rubbed with a greasy substance, no matter how inert.

Just as heat, rubbing, anointing with oil and purging were regarded as standard components in the armoury of self-medication, so too was 'swealing', 'swaling' and 'swaying'. As one rubbed a joint or purged a humour, so one 'swealed' or 'swayed' a swelling. It is a word which one encounters time and again in traditional medicine, and seemed to represent an essentially arcane, semi-magical procedure. Cancers and lumps were the objects most commonly 'swealed', though I have yet to find anyone who can tell me exactly how it was believed to be done. The word itself most likely derives from the Old English *swaelan*, which means to burn, and probably forms a cognate with the 'sweeling' of dead grass and sooty chimneys.[15] Medically, the word generally implied the presence of a substance or procedure which would 'burn away' a tumour.

A correspondent who grew up in Birmingham informed me that he encountered the use of the word by a local doctor in the 1930s. This man was, as far as my correspondent could recall, a regular trained physician who did not approve of surgery, and was renowned among the people of the locality for his ability to 'sweal away' growths by a secret method. How far this doctor genuinely mixed ancient folk cures with more orthodox medical techniques, or how far he simply tried to describe modes of treatment in a language which his patients could understand, I have been unable to ascertain.[16] Unfortunately, my respondent could not remember the doctor's name or details, apart from the fact that he was an old man who always wore a starched wing collar, so it has not been possible to check his licence or status within the Birmingham medical community of the day.

Swealing, however, does seem to have been a branch of medicine which could often be handed over to professionals, either to skilled folk-swealers, or even conventionally trained doctors. One must remember that D.H. Lawrence speaks of swealing towards the end of *Sons and Lovers*. When Mrs Morel is found to have an inoperable cancerous growth, the family ask the attending physician whether it is possible for him to sweal it away, and by way of offering comfort, the doctor says that he will try.[17] While I was gathering information in the late 1980s, two contemporary references to swealing came to my attention, both in the context of orthodox medicine. The first came from a retired surgeon who had practised in the Liverpool area and who informed me that it was not unknown for colleagues to explain to a patient being treated for a lump or tumour that they would sweal it away. The second instance related to a neighbour of my mother's who had to be admitted into the Salford Royal

Do you
believe in
Herbs?

If not, why not?

Sit down and read
our Lectures, etc.,
through, and be
convinced.

If you do not require
the book, pass it on
to a friend, and we
will thank you and
present you with
another free of
charge.

We do!

and we find
that

Herbs Cure

when

Minerals fail.

The image of a wise herbalist in seventeenth-century costume –
perhaps Nicholas Culpeper – contrasted with the poisonous
'Minerals' used by modern doctors. W. Aloysius Browne and W.H.
Browne, *The 'Walpole' Botanic Guide to Health* (Southampton,
c.1930), p.44. (Kindly presented to the author by Mrs Janet
McCallum, of Burscough, Lancashire, and now in his collection.)

Infirmary for the treatment of a growth. My mother remarked
that modern doctors were so good that they would probably
be able to 'sweal away' her neighbour's infirmity.[18] Old
words, like old cures, die hard.

The cures in which folk medicine came to place its
greatest faith, indeed, were those which hinged upon its
fundamental precepts of purging, 'natural' treatments, and
self-medication: namely, herbs and water.

Herbal cures possess a written vernacular ancestry going back to the Tudor herbals discussed in Chapter 2, while the almanacs and poor men's guides to 'physicke' had helped disseminate their ideas among ordinary people. By the late Victorian age, however, a branch of fringe medicine known as 'medical botany' had established itself, and was especially strong in the mill towns of the north-west. These included the 'Coffinites', mentioned in Chapter 3. And as Eunice Schofield has pointed out, there were some three hundred and fifty-one Herbal practitioners listed in *Kelly's Directory* for Lancashire in 1909 – mainly in Bolton, Blackburn and Oldham.[19] As the 1883 edition of *Consult Me* expresses it:

'Vegetable substances afford the mildest, most efficient and most congenial remedies to the human frame'.[20]

They were contrasted with the 'barbarous system of bleeding, salivating, cauterising and blistering' used in conventional medicine. Herbal remedies were also good because their 'mildness' occasioned no shocks to the system. Yet it should be understood that when speaking of herbs, most of their advocates generally meant garden or common hedgerow plants, and not narcotics and opiates, which most practitioners were quick to condemn as 'poisons'. Generally speaking, such botanical practitioners did not use the word 'herb' for just any plant which grew in the ground, but reserved it for those drugs which possessed a 'soothing' as opposed to a 'violent' action. But one soon perceives such a classification to be little more than a table of the individual herbalist's likes and dislikes.

Virtually all of my respondents concurred in their great faith in herbal treatments, and many were willing to recommend their favourites to me. Several people provided me with recipes for elaborate herbal brews, while one Salford lady sent me the complete contents of her grandmother's own herbal notebook, which contained recipes going well back into the nineteenth century.[21] Such a firm faith in herbs shows how recent, relatively speaking, was the Victorian industrial worker's connection with the fields and an agricultural life,

The Walpole Botanic Dispensary, 133–134 St Mary's Street, Southampton. Browne and Browne, *The 'Walpole' Botanic Guide to Health* (Southampton, *c*.1930), p.5. (Author's collection.)

and for those town-dwellers unlikely to gain access to the open fields, many corner shops and general dealers came to purvey packets and bunches of herbs. As Dr Anne Secord has so clearly shown, botanical clubs, which made a serious high-level study of plant taxonomy, distribution, and medicinal 'virtues', were very popular in the north of England during the Industrial Revolution, especially in the Manchester area.[22] Their Sunday outings in the fields and on the Pennines to collect and study specimens formed a major component in working-class self-education, and no doubt fed a great deal of botanical knowledge into working-class life in general. My own grandfather was a late, second-hand beneficiary of this tradition.

But by the end of the nineteenth century, the great majority of industrial workers had lost any regular access to the countryside. Consequently, many firms of 'medical botanists' came to issue substantial books which frequently served the combined functions of teaching the reader some medical botany while at the same time advertising the company's wares. *The 'Walpole' Botanic Guide to Health,* of *circa* 1930, forms a superior specimen of this genre. Written by Aloysius and Henry Browne, who seem to have been the proprietors of the company, this elegantly produced and illustrated 130-page publication uses a subtle mixture of apparent public-spiritedness and gentle emotional blackmail to promote its wares.

'Dear Reader; TREASURE THIS BOOK', it commences, and beseeches the mother to 'save the life of her little ones' by carefully following its precepts. The book is illustrated with a lugubrious pair of portraits of the authors, their dispensary in Southampton, and the advertisement of free consultations to the poor. 'No poisons or injurious drugs [are] used', one is informed, before the work commences with a description of a wide variety of diseases and how they can be cured by 'Walpole' herbs.[23]

Coughs, one is told, can be occasioned by worms and need purging, while epilepsy is often the result of 'obstructed circulation'.[24] Though not mentioning the actual word 'humours', it nonetheless mentions their traditional attributes, and ascribes most diseases to imbalances and obstructions. Blood purification is deemed a cure for a wide range of maladies including acne and falling hair, while the plant burdock is extensively recommended as a cleansing agent for the blood, and for scurvy, eruptions, and kidney complaints.

77

Lugubriously Learned: 'W. Aloysius Browne, F.N.A.M.H.; F.Sc.S., etc. Free Advice by post daily'. Aloysius Browne claimed forty-six years' experience as a 'Botanic Practitioner'. Browne and Browne, *The 'Walpole' Botanic Guide to Health* (Southampton, *c*.1930), p.6. (Author's collection.)

In a little glossary of technical, medical and botanical terms, the word 'Alterative' was given to those substances which 'purify the blood and cleanse the system of morbid matter'. Similarly, the term 'Anti-bilious' was used for substances which 'corrected the bile'.

Foodstuffs were also held to play a crucial role in disease processes, and the virtues of 'strong' and 'mild' foods were shown to have specific medical consequences. Pregnant women, for instance, should live on a mild diet if they wanted an easy delivery, for red meats hardened the skull bones of the child.[25] Cancer was also ascribed to diet and the over-consumption of meat; the reader is informed that Australia has both the highest meat consumption and the highest cancer rates in the world.[26]

Thoughtfully Therapeutic: C.W. Browne, A.N.A.M.H., 'Certified Botanic Specialists in Chronic Diseases. No POISONS or INJURIOUS DRUGS USED'. Browne and Browne, *The 'Walpole' Botanic Guide* (Southampton, *c*.1930), p.7. (Author's collection.)

The firm's 'Herbal Blood Mixture' was recommended against many of these maladies, for it purified the blood, and gave it life and vitality.[27] Several references to 'Spring Cleaning Medicines' reinforce the virtues of good purges.

The book has no truck with academic medicine – especially surgery, which it generally castigates. On the subject of cancer treatment by surgical means, it strikes the *coup de grace* at academic medicine by including a quote from the *Reminiscences* of Dr Robert Bell, the Victorian surgeon who confessed that operations for this disease did not always effect a permanent cure (and who is further mentioned on p.130).[28] Although by 1930 the law was beginning to move against those who advertised cures for cancer and consumption, it was still possible to imply relief for these conditions when the blood was purified with the correct herbs:

'In cancer you must absolutely alter the whole character of the blood and general system, and especially to flush out the lower bowels daily with an enema'.[29]

Such a quotation would not have been out of place amongst the writings of Hippocrates or those of diet reformers and naturopaths like Stanley J. Lief (who will be discussed in Chapter 6).

The firm customer preference for herbal simples, purges and self-medication was something to which many enterprising manufacturers of proprietary medicines gave ready acknowledgement. Though there have been some recent studies on the usage of patent medicines by the Victorian and Edwardian working classes, much of the attention has been devoted to the preparations as articles of commerce.[30] Relatively little attention has been paid to what a potential customer believed a particular patent medicine would do, and how its actions would conform to firmly held precepts about health and sickness. Yet when one reads the advertisements for these preparations, one is struck by the conservatism of the tradition to which they claim to belong, its humoral character, and its stress on cleansing. Many purveyors of these medicines advocate the 'good old cures', and adamantly castigate the 'poison-mongering' physicians who were also their commercial rivals. When patent medicines *did* capitalise on innovation, it was usually in the proclaimed discovery of a 'wonder herb' from the jungles of Africa (like the Umckaloabo root quoted by Eunice Schofield)[31] or from the American Indians, rather than the new 'magic bullets' of aspirin, caffeine or Salvarsan produced in the German medical research laboratories at the turn of the century.

To a customer for whom fragments of humoral physiology still formed a part of medical thinking, Carter's 'Little Liver Pills', 'Bile Beans' and 'Blood Purifiers' possessed an immediate logic and sense of purpose. If the blood was generated in the liver, then the liver – along with the bile and the blood – needed regular purging. Kidney and stomach pills would likewise fortify and strengthen those organs, especially in spring. Just as every wise patent medicine manufacturer knew that only a thick, glutinous 'mixture' could 'cut the phlegm' of a bronchial cough, so he knew that advertisements couched in the language of purging and sluicing the humours would also make good sense to a potential customer.

Many patent medicine manufacturers, like the medical botanists, issued substantial booklets which aimed to promote their wares while at the same time 'explaining' diseases to their readers. Some of these publications were blatantly aggressive in tone, and aimed to make the patient realise even before he or she got beyond the front cover that life was fast slipping away. Almost uniformly, however, these books employ the language, imagery and even illustrations of simplified classical medicine.

Fennings' Everybody's Doctor: or when ill, how to get well was published in 1864, and was still being issued, with only minor modifications, at the turn of the century. Its aim was to describe a variety of diseases, and then prescribe a range of Fennings' patent preparations for their cure. The immemorial, classical character of medicine to which it aspired was immediately exemplified by the cover illustration: a man in ancient Greek toga, holding the Asclepian serpent and staff, offers a cup to a woman lying in a Victorian sickroom. The companion illustration at the end of the book shows a similarly attired bearded sage offering relief to a man in stiff collar and whiskers (see pp.28–29).[32]

All artistry apart, the book goes on to list the illnesses which it purports to cure, including cholera and diphtheria; and in case anyone was inclined to underrate the Asclepian wisdom, it aggressively warns: [33]

'One fourth of the human population die before they are seven years old and one half before their seventeenth year. Of every one hundred persons born, not one dozen live to be fifty years of age, not more than half a dozen to sixty, and only one survives the sixty-fifth year.'

> 19 Hargrave St-
> Little Coates
> Grimsby
> Lincs
>
> Dear Sir
> Herewith I send you photo of our boy aged 14, who has suffered from hæmophilia and synovitis of the knee, and who had to use crutches for the last three years.
> He commenced taking your remedies in April 1924, and by August was so much improved as to be able to walk without crutches.
> We are continuing treatment, and hope to be able to report further improvement shortly.
> Thanking you very much for your help and advice
> Yours truly
> T. Blagg

T. Blagg's testimonial letter regarding the botanical cure of their fourteen-year-old son of a curious condition of the knee in 1924. Browne and Browne, *The 'Walpole' Botanic Guide to Health* (Southampton, *c*.1930), p.114. (Author's collection.)

Although such figures would have been fairly accurate for 1864, when the original Preface to the book was written, they would not have been for the last decade of the century, when the copy which I examined was printed. The increase of life expectancy would still only have been small, but it would have been significant.

The pathology offered to account for the diseases discussed by Alfred Fennings is as classical, in a debased

The boy on crutches, prior to treatment – and without crutches, after treatment with 'Walpole' herbs between April and August 1924. Note the identical hair, suit, tie and photographic back-drop. Only the crutches have disappeared. Browne and Browne, *The 'Walpole' Botanic Guide*, pp.115–116. (Author's collection.)

way, as the woodcuts of Asclepius. Blood figures prominently, being the cause of many disorders. Boils and eruptions, for instance, are the products of overheating the blood with too stimulating food, while even toothache could result when the blood was 'heated by too free living'.[34]

The classical doctrine of temperaments is also evoked, as when it is stated that Bilious persons (that is, those in whom Bile predominates) are especially prone to erysepilas. Such persons, moreover, are generally recognised by certain external characteristics, such as dark hair and eyes, possibly deriving from their Black Bile. Hysteria is also explained in accordance with the classical doctrine as a disease of women, to which frustrated spinsters were especially prone: 'Married life, with a few children, is a capital cure for hysterics.'[35] The conservatism of the book, and tendency to discuss diseases which were no longer a menace by 1900, is occasionally mitigated by some reference to slightly more up-to-date medical topics. Scarlet fever is spoken of as caused by animalcules (the old name for bacteria), though even here the pathology is more in keeping with the scientific ideas of the 1860s rather than the 1890s.[36]

Great stress is placed upon 'hidden diseases' and how special medicines were needed to seek them out. Disease is very much the malicious predator, lurking in the body ready to strike, and best offset by Fennings' branded medicines. Because Fennings' dealt in 'secret remedies' and would not reveal the contents of their concoctions, they were obliged to pay the government patent medicine stamp tax on their products. Like many other manufacturers of secret remedies, however, they used this stamp to advantage, implying that it was a government mark of approval for their products, and sternly warning readers of the book to buy only authentic Fennings' preparations, with the official stamp, 'to counterfeit which is a Felony'.[37]

The Fennings medicines sold were limited to a range of wonder preparations, which could (like most other patent medicines) each cure a dozen or more maladies. For 'hidden diseases', cholera, or any digestive problems, one was recommended Fennings' 'Stomachic Mixture'. There was also an 'Aperient Powder' and several others, which together could defend any family from all sickness, seeking out hidden diseases before they could strike. As a child, I clearly remember being given Fennings' 'Little Healer' pills by my mother.

Patent medicines, in spite of their popularity, were not cheap. Fennings' preparations, for instance, sold for around one shilling and threepence in the 1890s. Similarly, Walpole's Botanic Remedies cost between ninepence and two shillings and sixpence in the 1920s, while Beecham's Pills went for two shillings and sixpence, though advertised as 'worth a guinea a box'.[38] Considering prevailing wage levels during the period before World War I, this was a substantial outlay. When Tressell's journeyman house painters received between five pence and seven pence per hour,[39] and 59% of the working population earned less than twenty-five shillings per week, a box of pills could cost 10% of the family income, or half the weekly rent.[40] Though one might argue that such prices aimed more at lower-middle-class pockets, the popularity of patent medicines among working people was confirmed by many of my respondents, as well as writers like D.H. Lawrence. One way around the cost problem was that followed by the Middleton druggist Edward Lundie Smith, who sold Beecham's Pills repacketed at four for a penny. Though medicines sold in this way would have worked out more expensive in the long run, it made them accessible to people on very low incomes.[41]

The cleansing power of water was also ascribed an almost universal efficacy in popular therapeutics. Though some of this popularity derived, no doubt, from water's plentifulness, cheapness and powers of dissolving, one also suspects that something might well have come from its significance as an anointing agent. Water, after all, was the traditional agent of baptism, could be made holy by blessing, and was the substance with which both Jesus Christ and John the Baptist washed away bodily and spiritual sickness.[42] To a people familiar with the Gospel healing miracles, water was invested with many powers of cleansing. Many people to whom I have spoken have emphasised this aquatic power in folk medicine, especially as water (like herbs) was an ideal agency for self-medication. The Victorians, on all levels, were often great water-drinkers, especially after good piped supplies had become available, and the cult of hydrotherapy which arose during the middle years of the nineteenth century was a direct response to the idea that sufficient water could wash away any disease.[43] The medicinal virtues of water were thought to derive in part from the simple substance itself, and in part from the natural mineral salts that were often dissolved in it.

Hydropathy in its organised and influential form, however, began with Vincenz Priesstnitz, a charismatic Silesian (Austrian) peasant, who in the 1820s had noticed how sick animals fasted and tried to drink and dowse themselves with water. After Priesstnitz cured his own potentially crippling leg injury by a similar regimen, he initiated the famous

'Water Cure' at Grafenburg. This was no mere passive ingestation of local mineral springs, as was already the custom at Baden Baden, or Bath, but the strategic assault of the sick body with gallons of pure, plain water, taken internally or by a variety of exterior cold compresses or powerful jets. Unlike the old spas, Grafenburg under Priesstnitz used water alone: there were no mercurial physicians dosing the patients with pills, or supper parties in the evenings, where piles of meat and oceans of claret undid by night what the water had done by day. As Europe's first 'health farm', Grafenburg kept the patients' noses to the curative grindstone, and for many it worked – at least in the short term, as will be discussed in due course. Indeed, the Grafenburg régime was soon imitated across Europe and America, most notably in England at Harrogate, Buxton, and at Charles Darwin's oft-frequented Malvern.

For those people too poor to sample the exotic springs of Grafenburg or even Buxton, wholesome alternatives were available. The pure, soft waters of the Pennines which came to supply the drinking water of many industrial towns by 1900, and shortly afterwards the waters of Lake Thirlemere, were held to be excellent scourges of sickness. They could be drunk in large quantities, as well as used to wash the body externally. My grandfather neatly summed up this philosophy when he claimed, 'that which will wash outside the body will also wash inside'. He was a devoted, lifelong water-drinker, scarcely ever touching alcohol and only the occasional cup of tea. The regimen clearly did him no harm, for when he was admitted to hospital for a routine cataract operation at the age of ninety-one, he astonished the admitting physician by possessing a blank National Health treatment card. My mother and several of her friends swore by the consumption of warm Lake District tap water, which they asserted dissolved the fat deposits which build up around the heart.

One branch of unorthodox medicine which gained a firm footing in Victorian Lancashire was homeopathy. Starting in Germany in the 1790s, homeopathy was originally the product of a splinter group within the academic medical community, when Dr Samuel Hahnemann, an impeccably educated physician who had studied at Vienna, Leipzig and Erlangen Universities, argued that diseases were best cured with drugs producing similar symptoms (from the Greek *homoios*, the same), rather than those producing contrary symptoms.[44] This was, of course, quite against the prevailing orthodoxy in European academic medicine, which argued that diseases should be treated with allopathic drugs, which would produce contrary reactions to the symptoms produced by the illness. Homeopathy, however, had a clear lineage back to certain strands of thought in classical medicine. The homeopaths later developed the theory that the human body required five essential salts to keep health in proper balance, and it was in this form that later homeopathic practitioners came to elucidate their ideas. Homeopathy argued that its five simple salts – such as potassium phosphate and potassium sulphate – were essential to maintaining the correctly balanced functions of the organs. It claimed, moreover, that these salts gained in potency as the dose became progressively attenuated. In other words, a pinch of a simple salt in a bathful of water gave a more effective dose than the salt in its neat state.[45]

Homeopathic salts and preparations came to be sold through numerous outlets across the country, though gaining a major hold upon the north-west. Several regularly trained physicians came to practise it, in emulation of Dr Hahnemann, though their unconverted colleagues generally closed ranks against them. In the Council Minutes of the Liverpool Medical Institution for the 1850s, for instance, it was decided that doctors in the city who started to practise homeopathy could not be members of that very prestigious Institution.[46] The popular appeal of homeopathy is of course far from extinct today, and I shall say more about its current status in my concluding chapter.

Water cures and homeopathy had important features in common. Both were rooted in simple systems which tailored nicely into the obvious demand that a popular medicine must be wholly explicable to an uneducated person. Water cure or hydropathy gave one a sense of freshness outside as well as providing a comfortable internal image, as the good,

87

wholesome water unbunged heavy humours, sluicing out lurking poisons and dissolving predatory illnesses. Like the Great Flood of Noah, regular internal inundations could wash out nastiness in all its forms. Homeopathy complemented this imagery. Mild doses of simple salts, often mixed with copious draughts of water, were the very antithesis of the opiates, alkaloids, mercurial and antimonical drugs of the regular physicians. What is more, water and homeopathy were within the commonsensical grasp of every man and woman as well as being either cheap or else entirely free.

In the nineteenth-century medical context, however, homeopathy and hydropathy actually worked, and this factor contributed significantly to their popularity amongst working people. The success of these two systems of medicine in the nineteenth century owed much to the far from perfect state of academic medicine at this period, which had first disillusioned Dr Hahnemann. Though medicine had made great progress in terms of its scientific study of the human body, it was still a very defective art when it came to curing the sick. It is true that by 1890 germs could be recognised and correctly associated with specific diseases, but their action could not be stopped, nor the patient's life saved. Likewise, learned physicians were developing systematic knowledge about the functions of the brain and nerves, lymph and glandular systems, yet were still impotent in the face of insanity, diabetes and 'wasting diseases'. When an academically trained physician treated the sick, he still depended on a few practical procedures which had not drastically changed in years. Opium was still the principal pain-killer (though now given intravenously in the form of its active ingredient, morphine). Such heavy metal salts as arsenic, antimony and mercury were still administered to break fevers or to stop infections. While mercury could help to allay the symptoms of venereal disease, or arsenic moderate a fever, no doctor or pathologist could explain exactly how these drugs acted. Academic medicine, in short, still groped very much in the dark when dealing with actual cases of illness, and one can fully sympathise with those medical botanists, homeopaths and hydropaths who condemned the 'barbarous practices' of the 'poison-mongering' doctors.

Just as no regular physician knew exactly why or how certain drugs and minerals worked, it was all too well known that when these substances were used over prolonged periods, they were just as likely to kill the patient as was the disease which they were being used to combat. Two or three weeks of regular morphine injections could make one an addict for life. Mineral drugs such as arsenic and lead tended to do serious damage to body tissue, and many people were turned into wasted, permanent invalids by the prescription of such compounds by doctors of medicine. On the other hand, a hydropathic practitioner who prescribed nothing more than the drinking of many gallons of water per day, or the homeopath who gave minuscule doses of harmless domestic salts, could perform seeming miracles. Liberated from their daily doses of calomel, bismuth or mercury pills and given a 'good washing out', they sometimes showed instantaneous improvement. In this way, the Victorian professional invalid, who could not infrequently be a fairly healthy hypochondriac (as we shall see in Chapter 6) could be given a new lease of life, while even those people who were genuinely sick might appear to rally under the new régime. With the chronically sick, it would now be the disease which finally killed them, rather than the disease plus arsenic and mercury drugs.[47]

Although homeopathy and hydropathy started as middle-class medical novelties in the early and middle nineteenth century, their innate cheapness and simplicity soon ensured their adoption by the poor, especially when their basic precepts fitted so neatly into the self-administration preferences of popular medicine. By 1920, however, when academic medicine itself was in the throes of a clinical revolution, which was at last making it increasingly effective in practical terms, water cures and homeopathy were loosening their hold on the better off. Among the poor, on the other hand, who were both financially and culturally separated from the world of science and learning, the old favourites still retained their place. Just as the poor of the seventeenth century had imbibed the 'hand-me-down' obsolete medicine of classical antiquity at the first rise of science, so their descendants of the Edwardian era and beyond received the cast-offs of the early Victorian alternative practitioners. And because the poor had so few resources and no systematic training which enabled them to judge, they sometimes continued to make use of what they were given long after the original donors had largely given it up.

Indeed, one might almost say that the Medicine of the People is something of an archaeological dig of the mind, where many different levels of discarded cultural fragments relating to health and disease are picked up, preserved, and grafted onto an immemorial body of ideas. Yet, in spite of popular medicine's firm preference for simple self-medication, the great generality of people had to admit that in many cases, expert help in one form or another was often needed. This in turn forced them into the care of a variety of doctors, quacks, chemists, dentists and herbalists, who not only produced an incongruous meeting of different medical worlds and belief systems, but helped define the popular image of the medical expert.

5

Doctors, druggists, dentists and quacks

Though self-medication was a favourite principle of popular medicine, there was always an acknowledged need for specialist expertise when domestic resources failed. This need evoked a range of specialists varying in quality from the trained physician to the quack and nostrum pedlar. It is the purpose of this chapter to examine these alternatives, their relative popularity, and how reliable they were judged to be by potential patients and customers.

Doctors

At the ostensible head of the range of specialist options available to the ailing working-class person was the academically trained physician. By 1900, most of these men (and a handful of women) would have been the graduates of university medical schools and possessors of degrees such as Bachelor of Medicine, or Licentiates of the Royal Colleges of Physicians and Surgeons. They would have been trained in the scientific medicine of the day, in which it was held that disease was an organ-related condition. They would have seen the heart as a pump and not a furnace, and the blood as a complex organic substance that carried oxygen, and was of the same temperature in all healthy human beings, irrespective of age or sex.[1]

Germs would also have been seen as the causal agents behind most infectious diseases, as opposed to the miasmas, stinks or bad airs of the popular tradition. Some of the older generation of registered medical practitioners of the 1890s could well have been trained by a form of apprenticeship based on the conditions laid down in the Apothecaries Act of 1815, though most general practitioners under sixty would have spent at least part of their training in a collegiate institution. Irrespective of their precise mode of entry, all would have been members of the 'medical profession', as

91

defined and registered under the Medical Act of 1858.[2]

Like any other person who sold a skill or service a century ago, the doctor usually expected direct payment. Because a consultation was likely to cost at least sixpence and often several shillings, plus the cost of medicines, he was only usually resorted to after the Medicine of the People had failed. A family of four, subsisting on one pound per week, could not afford doctor's bills of five and ten shillings, especially if the follow-up calls were likely to double or quadruple this sum. When illness struck down the breadwinner in a family, the workhouse and its humiliation immediately sprang to mind, for a household lacking a wage saw a protracted series of doctor's bills as the last straw. Even though slum doctors knew the conditions in which their patients lived, and were frequently willing to collect payment by instalments, the doctor had to eventually obtain his fees, or else *he* would be in the workhouse.[3]

By the early 1900s, though, many doctors were at least part-employed or subsidised by provident societies and sickness and insurance clubs. Such an arrangement guaranteed both attention for the sick breadwinner in return for a standard weekly contribution, and a regular income for the doctor who no longer needed to rely exclusively on the efficiency of his debt collectors.[4]

Although a number of clubs and friendly societies were willing to insure individuals and families, it was not until 1911, with Lloyd George's National Insurance Act, that the state took upon itself the creation of a scheme whereby each breadwinner would contribute a compulsory weekly sum that would give him access to competent health coverage.[5] By 1911, therefore, breadwinners of families could be registered with a doctors' panel for medical treatment. Though the scheme had been strongly resented at first by the medical profession, who objected to the idea of being state employees, many doctors opted to work for the scheme, for it gave financial benefits which could help regularise a shaky private practice in a poor district. It has been said that it was this Act which took doctors off bicycles and out of pony traps, and put them into motor cars.[6] It was also the first legislative and practical step towards the foundation, thirty-seven years later, of a National Health Service. Lloyd George's reforms, following the Liberal landslide victory in the General Election of 1906, saw the first consistent action by the state to hold some responsibility for the health of its own workforce, and the access of ordinary people to the rapidly advancing power of scientific medicine. The situation had become all the more urgent in the wake of reports from the army medical authorities on the poor state of health of many of the volunteers going to the colours in the Boer War in 1899–1901.[7] This had been the first major war in which recruits had been subject to a proper medical examination, and the state of ill-health and undernourishment of its manpower alarmed Parliament. On the other hand, Germany – against whom Britain was to go to war in 1914 – had already operated a form of health service for working people for the previous twenty years.[8]

The great majority of hospitals of the period were still privately endowed charitable institutions. For most of the nineteenth century it had been necessary to obtain a recommendation or ticket of admission from a Poor Law Guardian or other responsible person even to be admitted to them. Persons with incurable diseases, or morally opprobrious diseases such as syphilis, were not generally admitted, or else were referred to institutions for the hopeless. Venereal cases went to the humiliating 'lock' hospitals. Most workhouses possessed hospital wings, though these again usually required a public act of self-degradation on the part of the patient before he or she was likely to be admitted.[9]

Fever and isolation hospitals were perhaps the easiest institutions to get into, for they were built and maintained at public expense for the express purpose of removing those persons with typhus, smallpox and terminal consumption out of the overcrowded home environment and containing the disease as a public strategy. The subject of one of L.S. Lowry's paintings is a visit of the Fever Van to a slum street, ready to bear away the infected person.

Mrs Elsie Oman was employed as a ward maid in the isolation hospital at Ladywell, Eccles, Lancashire, in the early

1920s, and left a vivid account of her life there. She described the hopelessness of most of the consumption patients, and how young men were likely to enter relatively healthy in the early stages of the disease, yet become emaciated and die as the months progressed.[10]

In the Edwardian period, and certainly by the 1920s, the medical profession knew quite accurately what consumption was, and how to recognise its bacteria under the microscope. It was also known how these bacteria were transmitted from person to person, by coughing fits and the expectoration of blood and mucus. This is what gave rise to so many 'No Spitting' signs in public places.[11] On the other hand, there was nothing that the doctor could do to cure the disease once it had gained a foothold, and the prognosis became fatal. All that could be done was to remove victims out of society and make them cough their sputum into disinfected tin mugs, thereby preventing the transmission of their 'mickeys', or germs, to others.[12] Not until the development of antibiotics in the 1940s, or some sixty years after Robert Koch in Berlin had first identified the bacteria, could consumption be at last cured and lives saved.

Mrs Oman described the dedication with which the staff on all its levels worked in Ladywell Hospital. She herself contracted an infection (though not tubercular) at one stage, which she was fortunate to survive. Even the staff were not immune, and the admired Nurse Williams died of consumption, which she had probably contracted from the patients.[13]

Although it is all too easy for us to accuse the Victorian and Edwardian medical profession – who were, in the long run, the creators of the modes of treatment employed – of being callous towards the poor, this was by no means the case. We must remember that in 1900 it was not considered to be the state's duty to look after the sick *en masse*. Over the course of the nineteenth century, both central and local government had recognised a political responsibility to encourage public health and incarcerate the criminally insane, but this policy was not to be extended to illness in general. Whilst the state provided a broad legislative framework within which scientific medicine could operate – such as registering qualified practitioners and framing the Public Health Acts – it was left to competent private individuals to organise the working details. Once qualified, the doctor had to make his own living as honestly as possible, and it was not the state's duty to pay him a salary if he chose to spend his career ministering to the destitute. Similarly, if private subscribers and Poor Law Guardians raised funds to open and endow a hospital, it was up to them to decide who was admitted to it. Even such rate-funded amenities as workhouses were ultimately accountable to the tax-paying middle classes who demanded that their penny rate levy not be spent in making life comfortable for the shiftless.[14] When Scrooge asked the charity collectors, 'Are there no prisons, are there no workhouses?' he was speaking for many members of the middle classes who, like good citizens, had already paid their taxes.[15] Victorian values admired individual moral responsibility, while at the same time insisting that the state's contribution be kept to a cost-effective minimum.

Only after the sickly state of the Empire's manhood had been exposed by the Boer War, and our physical capacity to maintain a hold on world power questioned, did the state feel obliged to act. Between 1907 and 1914 many innovations appeared, including the regular medical examination of schoolchildren and the granting of milk and food supplements to the young, along with the health insurance of their fathers.[16] The innovations had begun to bear fruit by 1914, though in the long run this improved state of health was probably responsible for sending hundreds of thousands of men to their death in Flanders.

Attitudes towards the medical profession on the part of working people themselves, therefore, were not likely to be clear cut or simple. It was generally agreed that doctors were 'clever' men, though by no means uniformly altruistic. Many elderly people spoke of the *hauteur* of slum doctors, and the way in which they addressed their patients as halfwits or malingerers. This is an opinion concurred with by various later writers, such as Robert Roberts, and the elderly people of Preston and Lancaster interviewed by Elizabeth Roberts.[17]

Many factors led to the image of awe created by the

formally qualified doctor practising in a working-class district, not least of which was the financial and social chasm which existed between him and his patients. In that strict social segregation which came with industrialism, it must have been hard to see as a friend the man who lived in a large house, employed servants, and ran a modest vehicle. In a district where the workers earned one pound per week and the foreman earned two pounds, the doctor with a thousand a year belonged to the world of the bosses, not the people.[18] Doctors, furthermore, like certain well-beneficed Anglican clergy, were the richest people that most working folk were ever likely to talk to, and in the popular mind phased into the hazy world of aristocracy, royalty, mill owners and all those lucky people who did not periodically starve. I remember an old Pendlebury man once saying to me that Oxford University was only for the likes of lords' sons, doctors' sons and similar well-to-do people. The social perceptions of the poor were narrow, and all men who wore clean collars and well-cut suits were seen as belonging to the same social group. And in so many ways they did, for on their various levels they were all 'gentlemen' – and in 1914 their sons automatically became commissioned officers.

Yet many doctors enjoyed considerable personal popularity and admiration from their patients.[19] In the late 1960s I worked for a while with a man whose grandfather, Dr Garden, had been a prominent Salford doctor around the turn of the century, and had been one of the first worthies of that city to exchange his coach and pair for a motor car. Like most successful physicians, he gave house calls and ran clinics free of charge for the poor, as well as running various children's charities. On the other hand, so my informant told me, grandfather could be a 'hard bugger', willing to send his chauffeur (who also doubled as his bill collector) around in the evenings to secure payment where necessary. In a world where medicine was as much a business as a humane service, one can fully appreciate the sound logic behind this apparent double standard.[20]

The superior status of doctors in the eyes of working people was brought home by the conduct of an elderly relative of mine, my aunt Jenny, who was born in the mid-

1890s, and for many years had acted as a cleaner to a local G.P. Though this lady was the scourge of petty officialdom and was ever ready to do battle to secure justice from anyone foolish enough to mistreat her, she always spoke with great respect about her medical employer. Doctors, after all, were gentlemen – a part of the human race for which many members of the working class always nurtured a curious affection. The behaviour of the fictional Hilda Ogden in Granada Television's *Coronation Street* towards her 'genteel' employer, Dr Lowther, in the mid-1980s, still reflects the old awe with which the good-hearted medical gentleman could be regarded even into our own day.

If a doctor was dedicated, kindly and civil (even while being a 'hard bugger'), he could enjoy a great local popularity. As a small child, I had vivid memories of the family doctor I was occasionally taken to see, Dr Abraham of Pendlebury, and of his blunt, humorous manner. Though he was then, in the mid-1950s, approaching retirement, I have since heard many stories about him from former patients. I remembered his dark consulting room overlooking a back yard, and the sepulchral waiting room before it. Irrespective of these drawbacks, however, and his reputation for being a rough handler during examinations, he made his patients laugh. My mother told me that when once consulting him on some minor malady, he greeted her by saying 'Well, I have not seen anyone as fit-looking as you walk through that door in years'. His blunt descriptions and swear-words endeared him to his patients and put them at ease in the nervous ambience of the consulting room. He once spoke of a man bent over with a bad back as 'Here's me head and me arse is coming', and while such phrases may not have been delicate, they were preferred to an aloof formality.

Another Pendlebury G.P. of the inter-war years, Dr Berry, enjoyed popularity from the way in which he championed local workpeople in dangerous occupations. He campaigned against the poisonous conditions prevailing in a local chemical factory which used noxious lead compounds, and let it be known that should his hat blow over the factory wall, he would not risk his own lungs in trying to retrieve it.

General practitioners made more house calls and ordered more treatments in their patients' homes than they do today. This was partly the product of much more restricted hospital resources, and partly from the fact that medical treatment was far less technological than it is today. The only valid reasons for admitting a person to hospital before 1940 was either to isolate an infectious case, or else provide specialist treatment and intensive care for surgery. Surgery itself was much more limited in scope than it is today, being mainly concerned with amputations, hernias, complex fracture reductions and external cancer removals.

Appendectomies were becoming more widespread, however, and the development of anaesthetics, antiseptics and blood transfusion had greatly extended the surgeon's capacities in little more than a couple of generations. Yet none of this surgery demanded much in the way of elaborate equipment apart from a case of instruments, a clean environment and great personal dexterity on the part of the operator. Surgeons were still very much craftsmen who worked as virtuosos, not as team leaders. Not until the surgical revolution which followed World War II, with open heart, spare part and transplant surgery, did the operating theatre change from being a well-scrubbed room into a laboratory.

When surgery was still technically simple, and there were still no antibiotics or regulatory drugs available, a protracted after-care was inevitable. A major operation could be followed by many months of hospitalised convalescence, and if the patient lived in an overcrowded insanitary slum without correct hygiene or even hot water, the surgeon knew he was wasting his time sending them home before recovery was well under way. If he did, all the good work was likely to be undone by well-meant but incompetent domestic nursing. Many wealthy people, who could have special sickrooms prepared and nurses engaged, would have their operations at home rather than submit to the indignity of a public hospital, for when the surgeon required little technological back-up, one clean room was as good as another.

Surgery was avoided as much as possible, not only because it was much more dangerous than it is today, but because after-care was so protracted and potentially ruinous to a poor family. People would prefer to suffer in silence, receive whatever medical treatment the G.P. could offer, and sometimes resort to quack preparations, rather than 'submit to the knife'.

Hospitals, and especially surgical wards, frightened people for many good reasons. Not only were they generally long-stay places, but many people came out feet first. Having to submit to the stern discipline of matrons and nurses also terrified people, for one was in a place with all the regimentation of the factory, without any of the comforts of home. The hospital was, after all, the antithesis of the cosy domestic hearth beloved by most people. Aspects of this attitude survived in the *Carry On...* British comedy films of the 1960s and early 1970s, which frequently depicted patient, doctor and nurse sequences. The male patients were invariably treated like naughty boys by the senior nurses and like fools by the senior doctors, while the patients in their turn did whatever they could to evade the stern discipline with their secret smoking, drinking and horseplay.

Perhaps it was because of this fear of entering hospital on the part of patients that many surgeons did perform certain operations in working-class homes, especially if the surgery was simple and did not involve the internal organs. Elizabeth Roberts interviewed several people in north Lancashire who had known of such operations performed upon members of their own families before 1920, but was of the opinion that domestic surgery ceased to be performed after that date.[21] My mother had a friend, however, whom she could remember having her tonsils removed at home in Pendlebury around 1931. From what my mother could recall, the operation was performed in a back bedroom prepared beforehand in accordance with the doctor's strict instructions. The tonsillectomy was performed by the family G.P., Dr O'Grady, though it is unlikely that anything more serious would have been attempted outside a hospital at this late date. A tonsillectomy did not involve major external incisions or elaborate post-operative dressings, and for this reason could be attempted in the home.

Midwifery was still being performed at home, at least for straightforward cases, well after 1931, and though not always requiring the attendance of a physician, was coming to be the province of the trained midwife or District Nurse, as opposed to the folk accoucheuses who still predominated up to World War I.[22]

Popular attitudes to doctors and formal practitioners of scientific medicine were, therefore, coloured by many factors. The alien, middle-class world of the consulting room, the high charges, and the frequently authoritarian attitude of doctors often put people off. On the other hand, even the firmest adherents of herbs and self-medication with whom I spoke agreed that doctors were life-savers, and indispensable in serious cases. Perhaps this attitude has developed or at least drawn strength from fifty years of socialised medicine and the greater ease of access to physicians, along with a massive relaxation of the old social boundaries, so that ordinary people feel less threatened by the professional men and women whom the state and, more recently, Health Trusts, now employ to heal them.

Druggists and dentists

The half-way house towards scientific medicine for the working man or woman in 1900 was the chemist or druggist. Most practitioners had been through a fairly elaborate training by this date, comprising a combination of apprenticeship and classroom work. The Pharmaceutical Society, founded in 1841 and incorporated in 1843, provided academic standards, and ensured that its members were familiar with such subjects as chemistry and medical dispensing.[23] Though the chemist was not legally supposed to make house calls or prescribe on his own account, there was nothing stopping him recommending either his own or else some commercially manufactured pharmaceutical preparations to persons asking for a cough bottle or a rub. Chemists had two great attractions to the working-class patient: they were much cheaper than the doctor, as well as being generally more approachable. The shop counter was a more familiar milieu than the mahogany-topped desk across which to seek advice. Chemists might be superior shopkeepers, but shopkeepers they were nonetheless, and could be approached more like the butcher or greengrocer.

The Lundie Smiths were a family of which several members (including two brothers) became chemists and druggists in the Manchester area around 1900. One of the brothers, after qualifying, went into practice in his own premises in the 1890s, working alongside his unqualified brother. Though Edward Lundie Smith never went on, like his elder brother, to take the qualifying examinations, he did become a skilled and successful druggist who in 1908 moved to the Manchester suburb of Moston and opened his own shop. Mr Edward Lundie Smith's daughter, the now late Mrs Georgina Kelly, very kindly gave me information about how the druggists' trade operated at the turn of the century, their relations with the local doctors with whom they worked closely, and how both medical and customer expectations changed over time up to her father's retirement in 1940.[24]

Edward Lundie Smith sold a wide range of medicines, some of which were his own special preparations, and others which were commercial pharmaceutical, patent and herbal substances. The business ran a popular line in herbal medicines (in accordance with customer demand), and Mrs Kelly recalled that the general price for most patent medicines was one shilling and threepence, though her father sold many pills remade up into packets of four for a penny. Mrs Kelly could never remember the sale of laudanum in her father's shop (which could not, in 1910, have been sold by an unqualified person), though chlorodyne was sold. Aspirin had become the principal domestic analgesic by 1914, and was itself a product of the new scientific pharmacy. The shop was run, like many other small businesses, as a family concern, and before 1914 Mrs Kelly (or Miss Lundie Smith) was already practised in weighing out salts and such substances for her father's mixes.

Many druggists and chemists ran their own special lines or remedies for such common maladies as coughs, constipation and indigestion. Black treacle and chlorodyne formed the basis of a popular cough syrup of Mr Lundie Smith's (it would also have had a purging effect), while a popular children's syrup was boiled up regularly in a large pan over the kitchen fire.

The limited pharmaceutical resources of many hospitals, and their dependence upon the manufactured products of local chemists who supplied them, became apparent from the activities of a friend and colleague of Mr Lundie Smith, who supplied Ancoats Hospital, Manchester, with his own burn cream. This gentleman also used the kitchen range fire to make up his cream, and on one occasion a fall of chimney soot came down into a fresh panful, only to get mixed in, and delivered in due course to the hospital. The soot-polluted cream, however, turned out to be more efficacious than the unpolluted form, for the hospital soon became desirous of having more of the 'new formula' burn cream. Such incidents demonstrate how close to cookery such pharmacy still was, while the druggist's willingness to sell his preparations by the cupful (as did Mr Lundie Smith with his cough mixture) reinforces the familiar domestic basis.

Mr Lundie Smith did not make house calls, though patients would come to the shop to seek his advice, while Mrs Lundie Smith ran a service for mothers and children, to deal with their particular medical needs. None of this 'consultancy' work seems to have been resented by local doctors, who frequently called into the shop, bought its proprietor's special preparations, and worked on friendly terms with the druggist.

A common sideline of the chemist and druggist was tooth extraction. Before the 1930s, few working people consulted professional dentists, or received any form of oral care beyond that of a simple extraction. Dentistry also remained a favourite bastion of self-medication, and where it did fall into professional hands, it usually fell into those of druggists or quacks. While I shall be dealing with commercial quack dentistry in the following section of the present chapter, something must be said here of the druggist-dentist and his clientele.

The dental health of most working people, according to the doctors and dentists I spoke to, was bad. A fondness for sugared foods, beers with a high sugar content, and sweet tea, represented some of the relatively cheap pleasures in an otherwise hard life. But like most other pleasures enjoyed by working people, sweetness was bought at a price. With the increasing availability of synthetic suction dentures in the 1930s, many people determined to cut their losses and have their natural teeth extracted (usually all at once) and replaced by a 'luvly set o' knashers'.[25] A medical man whose first professional appointment was in a Manchester hospital in the 1940s told me that he was astonished how many young working women sacrificed all their teeth to a pair of dentures before they got married. To girls working in the winding and weaving shed of the cotton mills, however, this decay process was probably hastened by drawing the broken threads through their front teeth, prior to mending a broken end.[26]

The colliers of Pendlebury (and no doubt elsewhere) practised a grim line in self-extraction in the Edwardian era. Both my grandmother and aunt Martha (born 1892 and 1893 respectively) spoke of their uncle, Bob Wroe, whose technique was to tie one end of a piece of fine packthread around the offending tooth, and the other around the doorknob of a heavy iron Dutch oven. On slamming the door shut, the offending tooth was wrenched out of its socket. The procedure saved money from the 'threepenny snatch' of the local chemist, though as Uncle Bob generously gave a 'meg', or halfpenny, hush-money to those children who had witnessed his roars, one suspects that little can have been saved in the long run.[27]

Many elderly people in the Swinton and Pendlebury district of north Manchester have spoken to me of Teddy Banks, who practised as a chemist on Bolton Road, Pendlebury, from the 1870s to the 1920s. He was a registered chemist and druggist, who had qualified in July 1871, and both dispensed for local doctors and sold his own proprietary brands and mixes.[28] He was described to me by a lady who recalled him in his later years after World War I as a tall, white-bearded, scrupulously clean man in a black frock coat. In addition to his pharmaceutical business, he practised lightning dental extractions, known to his victims as the 'threepenny snatch'.

To avail oneself of this service, one took a place in the customer queue in his shop. Upon the announcement that an extraction was required, Mr Banks would come from behind the counter, seat the patient in a chair (in full view of whoever was in the shop), produce a pair of forceps from up his sleeve, and do battle. Spitting blood, no doubt, the patient left the shop, and Teddy Banks resumed his place behind the counter to await the next customer. As it was possible to obtain a couple of pints of beer for threepence in the first decade of the century, however, one can understand why many colliers preferred the string and oven door for such a brief and anaesthetic-free service.

The fast extractions of Teddy Banks made it possible for the people who worked in the adjacent mills and were suffering from toothache to pop out for ten minutes to end their miseries. My grandfather, who went to work in Pendlebury's Acme mill (immortalised by L.S. Lowry) in 1903 as a 'lad' beneath his under-manager father, said that such quick errands of mercy to Teddy were often permitted by kindly charge hands.

Mr Lundie Smith also performed routine dental extractions, though he charged sixpence. This higher cost was perhaps justified by the greater prosperity of Moston as against the coal and cotton town of Pendlebury, along with the fact that his patients suffered their still anaesthetic-free ordeals in a back room, rather than in the open shop.

None of my respondents who discussed dental matters spoke of anything beyond simple extractions being performed until after World War II. This does not mean, of course, that fillings and more elaborate dental surgery were not performed upon working people, but that they were probably exceptional.

Extractions, usually prior to the fitting of false teeth, could also be performed in the patient's home. My grandfather decided, in the late 1920s, to have all his remaining teeth removed, and was operated upon for the extraction of more than twenty teeth in the back kitchen by a visiting dentist. Like most people, he decided that one major dental ordeal was all that he could face, and wanted them all out at once.

Because he was to receive the mercies of a cocaine local anaesthetic, however, it was necessary for the dentist to make two visits to remove a dozen or so teeth from the upper and lower jaws respectively on two occasions. The ordeal took place on consecutive Saturday afternoons, in the dinner-time interval between coming home from a morning's work and going to the rugby match. It was clearly a feat of endurance for both patient and dentist alike. 'He yanked 'em out like owd sticks', my grandmother recalled over forty years later, and 'chucked em over his [the dentist's] shoulder. I was sweeping up bad teeth for days after. One landed in a pudding.' Immediately following each operation, with jaws still streaming blood 'like a cannibal', grandfather dashed off to catch the start of the Swinton Lions match. Neither patient nor spouse could recall the operator's name and qualifications, though if he was administering cocaine with a hypodermic needle, he was most likely a qualified practitioner.

Both of my grandparents had their own versions of this Herculean feat, but grandmother's was the more detailed, possessing as it did the impartial detachment of the observer. Grandmother, indeed, was fascinated by anything medical, and loved nothing more than accompanying timorous neighbours on visits to doctors and dentists. She had lost her own teeth as a young woman, although she could never persuade her sisters Janet and Martha to part with theirs.

One possible reason why fillings were so rarely resorted to, apart from the considerably greater cost and time required for the operation, was the popular belief that once the 'rot' had got into a tooth, there was no real saving it. Decay in teeth was held to be similar to decay in woodwork. Once it had set in, all the paint and putty in the world could only delay the final disintegration, and with teeth, the final ordeal of extraction. Once the proprietary analgesics such as dabbing the tooth with oil of cloves or else sucking an aspirin had failed, it was better to suffer but once, and have it out.

Though hardly a professional treatment, the Welsh centenarian, John Evans, described a commonplace cure for toothache which consisted of probing the cavity with a red-hot needle. Though no explanation of this treatment was offered, it could well have had a cauterising effect on the tooth of anyone with sufficient nerve to try it.[29]

Mrs Beeton recommended Friar's Balsam, creosote and myrrh, though her more sophisticated home cure for toothache was to bite onto a silver coin sandwiched between the tooth and a scrap of zinc. This was said to generate a 'galvanic' current which would ease the ache, 'as if by magic'.[30]

It would be incorrect, however, to assume that amateur dentistry ended with the National Health Service. As recently as the late 1980s, two remarkable cases were related to me by dentists working in the same practice in Salford, north Manchester. One was of a man who had, indeed, filled his own decayed tooth cavities with the patent wall-repairing plaster Polyfilla. The other was a man who had carved his own set of false teeth from pieces of wood. Both efforts, one suspects, were the products of individuals who dreaded visiting dentists. Only when his unsterilised Polyfilla-filled teeth started to decay beneath their plaster casing was the first patient forced to seek the services of a professional dentist, there to find that he had inflicted so much damage on his cemented-together teeth that extractions were necessary. Although the dentist was willing to buy the other patient's home-made wooden teeth as a medical curiosity, he was told that they were not for sale.

What is extraordinary about some of the amateur dentistry which I have encountered, such as oven doors, red-hot needles and Polyfilla, is that it must have inflicted more suffering than a visit to a professional dentist. On the other hand, in an age when money was scarce, home dentistry was free of charge. Perhaps more importantly, it left the patient in complete control, which must have done something towards allaying the dread with which even brave men contemplated a visit to the dentist. The patient could brace his own nerves before slamming shut the oven door, or grip tightly onto the pair of pliers before jabbing the red-hot needle into the cavity as he stood before the mirror. The compromise solution, however, was to visit the quack dentist, who not infrequently performed 'lightning' extractions free of charge as a crowd draw prior to selling his medicines.

Quacks

Medical quackery is as old as medicine itself, and it might be plausibly argued that before the nineteenth century there was little to choose, in practical terms, between the quack and the regular physician. Though the regular doctor possessed a knowledge of scientific anatomy, and could read Hippocrates and Galen in Greek, his standard therapeutic procedures were still little more than shots in the dark. And since the founding of the academic Royal College of Physicians in 1518, doctors had been hounding quacks, though quackery proved to be fully up to the fray in terms of resilience.

With the increasing efficiency and legal regulation of the medical profession in the late nineteenth century, the onslaught against quacks, and their exposure, became a matter of law. As the Medical Act of 1858 (irrespective of its loopholes) had made it an offence to claim to be a qualified medical practitioner if one was not, prosecutions could become more systematic. In 1879 Dr Walter Rivington published a critique of his profession, including a section dealing with quacks.

After the passing of the Medical Act, people who now illegally called themselves 'doctor' were liable to a fine of £20 at the first offence, and Rivington mentions several, including a bogus 'Dr' Shaw of Bolton and a homeopath of Accrington, who were hauled up before the courts. Even more duplicitous was John William Foster, who simply assumed the credentials of a genuine but deceased physician of the same name who had not, by some oversight, been removed from the register at his passing away.[31]

But the most alarming of Rivington's cases were not those exposed for the misuse of formal medical titles, but the ones which involved empirics, quacks and folk healers working in a popular tradition. These were the men who peddled their wares amongst the poor, and were what may be called the 'quacks of the people'. These included the cancer curer who misdiagnosed a Spanish sailor's femoral hernia for a cancer of the groin and treated it with corrosives to burn it away. By the time the sailor received proper surgical treatment, his abdominal wall had decayed away and he was dying

A fairground mountebank of *c*.1600, complete with exotic dress, a case of drugs and a monkey. Henry Morley, *Memoirs of Bartholomew Fair* (London, 1859), p.284. (Author's collection.)

from multiple complications. The quack even escaped prosecution, for if one did not pretend to be a doctor, then the patient was held partly responsible for what he was willing to have done to him.[32] While it was illegal to pretend to be a doctor, the law was still unclear about how it should act concerning persons who did not claim such qualifications and whose victims willingly received their treatment.

In June 1875, a prosecution was successfully brought

'In the next place I recommend to you my incomparable Balsam...'
Another early seventeenth-century quack, with box, monkey and
clown. Henry Morley, *Memoirs of Bartholomew Fair* (London,
1859), p.150. (Author's collection.)

against one Mr Bigwood of Corsham (Wiltshire?), who
claimed not to be a physician, but a 'Licensed Botanist'.
Bigwood was very much a folk practitioner who in May that
year had reluctantly (or so he claimed) taken on the case of a
terminal consumptive who had been given up by the doctors.
What is remarkable about Bigwood is the way in which he
spoke of disease and health, for he said of his deceased
patient,

> 'But I did not think that I should raise him, for he had
> no blood in him. I told him that his liver did not throw
> any blood, and that it was very dry. I thought by his
> countenance that his liver did not throw any blood, as
> he looked as sallow as death. I sent him a bottle of
> medicine next day which contained seven different
> sorts of herbs. They were herbs governed by the Sun.
> These herbs strengthen the heart, which I wished to do.
> I work on a botanist's scale of astrology'.[33]

How many remnants of classical medicine are there here? The primacy of blood which was 'thrown' by the liver; dryness associated with death; seven herbs, a lucky number and the number of the seven classical planets, governed by the life-giving Sun, and astrology. Bigwood claimed to run an extensive trade selling his herbs for all kinds of cures 'all over the country', and treated fits, chest, heart, lungs and liver. With such a postal business, one is tempted to wonder how far quack medicine moved into new dimensions following the creation of the excellent postal system of the Victorian age. Rowland Hill's Penny Post, stamps and the railways had made it possible, by 1875, to send letters and small packages from one end of the country to the other in a couple of days.

Although Bigwood was probably a well-meaning folk quack who had shrewdly recognised the possibilities of easy communication, quackery could also descend to the overtly criminal, especially when victimising the very poor. There was the reported case of the travelling Irish quack who went to prison for twelve months for terrifying people with his imaginary new disease of which he foretold an epidemic. This was 'wolf of the liver', which was eating people up if they did not use his exclusive medicine.[34] One notes that it was the liver – the fundamental organ of classical physiology – that was being eaten up.

Quackery had always utilised the exotic, realising that a wonder cure from a far-off land, peddled by a doctor boasting grandiloquent and unverifiable qualifications, was more likely to succeed than a plain man selling a plain cure. Though there were quacks of fixed abode, who took premises and operated mail-order businesses, such characters had, by 1900, blended into the world of quasi-respectable patent medicine makers and urban botanists. The real quack was essentially a man of the road, and while he had become virtually extinct by 1920, he left a vivid legendary history behind him. 'Physician' Vilbert, the itinerant pedlar of love philtres and other nostrums from his box, represents a rural version of the genre in Hardy's *Jude the Obscure* (1896), while several of my respondents could recall quacks of various types on the northern markets before 1914.

My grandfather never forgot 'Dr' Sequah, whom he had seen on the market grounds of Pendlebury, Farnworth and Salford. Sequah was an itinerant who most likely moved on a fairly wide circuit, reappearing in the same towns every month or so. He peddled a variety of secret remedies, all of which he claimed to derive from the Red Indians of North America, and which were sold as part of an elaborate cowboys-and-Indians medicine show. My grandfather remembered Sequah wearing the head-dress of an Indian chief, with his face made up, and a team of accomplices who were supposed to be his braves. The performance would take place on a platform before a large booth or tent, to the raucous strains of a small brass band.

Upon making his grand entrance and securing a large crowd, the 'doctor' would invite those suffering from toothache to come up to the front for a 'lightning painless extraction'. The victim was taken behind a small screen at the back of the stage, and since no anaesthetic was administered, the brass band would strike up at full blast to deaden the screams. After a number of extractions had been performed, and the crowd had swelled to capacity, the real business of the day would commence, as 'Dr' Sequah's wonderful cures were brought out for sale. The hard sell would be moderated by songs, jokes, and tricks, in addition to the dentistry, to maintain the crowd's attention. My grandfather retained the most vivid recollections of this character from the Edwardian period, and said that his show was more entertaining than the music hall.

Yet Sequah was a quack, belonging as he did to the swan song era of quackery, before Lloyd George's rudimentary health service and World War I permanently altered the scope of life and medical expectation. How long he may have survived thereafter, or how long his imitators may have operated, it is impossible to say; though in about 1986 I was informed by a middle-aged man that his father had witnessed a travelling Red Indian medicine show at Maidstone, Kent, during the inter-war years.[35]

What must not be forgotten, however, is that 'Dr' Sequah was not just one man, but many, according to Mr B.R.

A street vendor of patent medicines, *c*.1880. (Radio Times Hulton Picture Library.)

Townsend's published account of 'Sequah', in *The Dental Record*.[36] Though it was claimed that an entrepreneur named Hartley, who may have received some formal medical training, was the founder of a registered limited company of the name 'Sequah' in 1883, it is apparent that this firm either trained up or permitted a number of other, presumably franchised, men to take shows around the country, peddling 'Sequah' quack medicines. Various people who witnessed Sequah shows in the 1880s and 1890s saw the 'doctor' variously dressed as an Indian, a cowboy and a man in ordinary attire, who was the centre of a Wild West circus entourage.[37] The enterprise, and the £100,000 capital which it possessed in 1895, seems to have been entirely British and in no way connected with the United States. One suspects that the 'Swamp Root' and 'Prairie Flower' medicines which it manufactured and sold were a shrewd way of capitalising on the craze for travelling Wild West shows and medicine shows, created by Wild Bill Hicock, Phineas Taylor Barnum, and others, that were current in the 1880s. During the 1880s, when at his height, Sequah took over theatres and public halls for his medicine spectaculars, before the company was liquidated in 1895. It is probable that my grandfather, who would not have been old enough to have witnessed an authentic Sequah, saw one or more of his imitators of the next decade. Sequah had clearly hit the popular imagination with great force in the 1880s and 1890s, and what could fill Lincoln Corn Exchange in the late 1880s[38] could still, in imitation, draw respectable crowds at a northern market in 1910.

Sequah produced penny booklets which aimed at explaining various diseases, and no doubt promoting Sequah preparations, in time-honoured quack style. Up to the time of writing, however, I have been unable to trace copies of these publications. Yet in all of the 'Sequah', or 'Sequaw', accounts which I have come across, both in printed and verbal sources, the same format remains: the Wild West show, the dental extractions, and the brass band as a prelude to selling the medicines. Like all astute quacks, Sequah knew the allure not only of distant, arcane medicine, but also of appeals to classical antiquity, and sometimes spoke of himself as being like Galen, coming back to cure the infirmities of the modern age.[39]

Several people have related encounters with itinerant tooth-drawers working as late as the early 1920s, either in imitation of the legendary Sequah, or operating on their own. One gentleman gave me a graphic description of such an operator who seems to have been of negro origin – 'A great big fella called Beni Mohammed Nanzu', who removed teeth on Cadishead market, Lancashire, around 1920.[40] The especially noteworthy feature about Beni Mohammed was that he used no instruments, but grabbed hold of the offending tooth with powerful fingers and worked it loose. One wonders if he ever got bitten.

Although I would not necessarily consider medical botanists as 'quacks' in the obvious sense, many of them did make use of that standard quack device, the patient's testimonial. Just as the theatrical Earl of Rochester in the seventeenth century raised laughs by declaring bogus testimonials in his quack doctor impersonations,[41] and Dr Sequah cured stooges from lameness and displayed discarded crutches, so the written testimonial figured prominently when quackery came to be propagated by the written word. Though it is impossible to determine the authenticity of particular testimonials, their value could become highly suspect once they began to rely on photographs.

The *'Walpole' Botanic Guide*, for instance, published two companion testimonial photographs of a boy who had enjoyed a wonderful cure for a swollen knee by the firm's remedies in 1924 (see pp.82–3).[42] Yet what immediately arouses suspicion about the authenticity of the pair of photographs is their similarity of detail. On the left-hand photograph, the boy is shown with a crutch and an injured left knee, while on the right, he is shown minus the crutch and bandage, standing up straight. On both pictures, however, the boy is wearing the same suit, tie and boots, while his hair is precisely of the same length and cut. Both pictures were taken against the same professional photographer's backdrop, with the boy standing in precisely the same place.

It is hard to imagine that anyone looking closely at these photographs can remotely believe that they are taken four months apart, as the accompanying testimonial letter claims. Such posed and sometimes retouched photographs were often used in medical quackery in the early twentieth century. I also possess another pair of photographs from an American publication of 1930, claiming to highlight the dangers of 'self-pollution' or masturbation. They depict one D.S. Burton of Pennsylvania, and were allegedly taken three years apart(see pp.128–9).[43] The first photograph shows Mr Burton as a man in his early twenties, dressed in the style of *circa* 1910. On the second photograph he has become a wreck of fifty, after three years' 'inveterate' practice of the 'vice'. This second photograph, however, almost qualifies as a painting, so heavily is it retouched. Lines and haggard creases have been added to the face, and grey streaks to the hair. All that remains of the first photograph to give the lie to the retouch is the precise outline of the head, the identical hairline and the clothes. But in an age still prone to invest near-gospel authority in the printed word or photographic image, one feels more inclined to credit the daring impudence of testimonial charlatans.

Rhymes, jingles and verses also enjoyed a wide quack vogue, as the charlatans knew the commercial value of simple songs that would stick in customers' minds. 'Dr' Sequah is alleged to have used one (amongst many) which went thus:

'There was a young girl who had her four
    teeth pulled out,
It made her wriggle and dance and shout,
She cried "Oh mother, come carry me out!
He's a wonder is Sequah the Doctor."' [44]

My father, born in 1907, could recall fragments of similar quack ditties, one of which I have been able to trace in its entirety, though he could only remember the first two lines:

'If you've pains in the back try Jujah,
    or a bilious attack, try Jujah,
For the measles or the dropsy
    or the chronic popsy-whopsy,
Try the celebrated medicine, Jujah.'

Although he could not remember its source, my father had known the jingle from childhood. I have since found that the song dates from a Pierrot show spoof on quack doctors, performed to holidaymakers in Bournemouth around 1890–1892, from whence it must have travelled to other shows and music halls.[45] Such songs – be they the wares of

CHOLERA,
SCARLET AND TYPHUS FEVER, PREVENTED OR CURED

TRADE MARK.

FENNINGS' FEVER CURER,

OR

FENNINGS' STOMACHIC MIXTURE

Will stop Diarrhœa, Loosenesses & Bowel Complaints with One Dose.

THE CELEBRATED REMEDY FOR THE PREVENTION OR CURE OF
Typhus or Low Fever, Cholera, Diphtheria, Scarlet Fever, Fluxes,
Yellow Fever, Influenza, Dysentery, Bowel Complaints, Windy
Spasms, Sore Throats, Griping Pains, Low Spirits, Bile,
Diarrhœa, &c.

Fennings' Stomachic Mixture will prevent persons catching Typhus or Low Fever, Scarlet
Fever, Cholera, Diphtheria and Yellow Fever, or will cure with two or three doses all these
fearful diseases. No case of Typhus Fever is hopeless with this remedy at hand. *See Fennings'*
Everybody's Doctor, page 8.

The value of such a Medicine may be surmised by the fact, that with two or three doses,
sometimes with only *one* dose, it will not only cure *Typhus* or *Low Fever, Cholera, Diphtheria,*
&c., but that if a dose be taken twice or three times a week, it will prevent a person catching
these dangerous Complaints, if in the neighbourhood or house.

Sold in Bottles 1s. 3d. *each, with full directions, by all Chemists.*

Observe the Proprietor's name, ALFRED FENNINGS, printed on the Government Stamp
round each Bottle, without which none are genuine.

'Fennings' Fever Curer', capable of curing anything from depression
to yellow fever. Note the classical imagery implying the medicine's
potency: the infant Hercules who, in his cradle, strangled two deadly
snakes. The last two lines of this advertisement imply that the
Government officially certified Fennings' undisclosed formula for
this mixture. *Fennings' Everybody's Doctor: or, when ill, how to get
well* (undated booklet, *post* 1863). (Author's collection.)

real quack doctors or music hall imitators – must have made a
major impression on their hearers if they were capable of
being picked up, albeit in fragmentary form, by schoolboys
twenty or thirty years later. The use of rhymes by quacks,
however, was only to be expected, as simple verses had been
used for centuries in orthodox medical training as an aid to
memory. I have encountered several memory rhymes in
Tudor medical texts, whereby they attempted to teach the
student the rules of bloodletting and the like.[46]

Religious or faith healing

One other aspect of medical specialism which was not necessarily part of quackery, yet which is outside the formal branches of the profession, is the art of the 'faith' or inspired healer. The annals of medical history contain accounts of many persons who were said to possess inexplicable medical gifts, many of which were religious in character. The seventeenth-century miracle healer Valentine Greatrakes, who 'stroked' away illness, was one of the most famous of these practitioners.[47] Greatrakes, who was an Irish landed gentleman of old family, would take no money, and regarded his gift as a divine one. Most other practitioners likewise claimed their gifts direct from God, or from fortunate accidents of birth. Seventh sons of seventh sons (and also daughters) were traditionally said to be so blessed.[48] Bone-setting and the manipulation of ailing joints, which was often thought to be a gift given to particular healers rather than a skill which was taught, comprised another folk specialism.[49] And like Valentine Greatrakes, these individuals invariably refused any recompense for their services.

Wart-charming is another folk 'specialism'. In 1988 I had a detailed conversation with (the late) Mrs Eileen Oliver, who was then 75, and who worked part-time on the kitchen staff of an Oxford College. A native of Norfolk, but having lived in Oxfordshire since childhood, Eileen told me that she was 'taught' wart-charming when she was 21, though she also recognised that she possessed a natural power for the art that came from within herself. At the start of her career she had touched the warts (and veruccas) with a new split hazel stick, which she would then throw away over her right shoulder; but later she found that merely touching the warts with her finger, while silently repeating certain words to herself, worked just as well. The warts invariably went away over the next two to three weeks. Although a church-goer, she did not see her gift in an especially religious context, though for some reason she could not explain, she would never 'touch' on a Friday (nor would she 'turn' beds on a Friday when she worked in domestic service.) Eileen was a straightforward, cheery and extremely active lady for her age, without the slightest 'magical' pretension, and volunteered her information to me privately, knowing my interest. And like Greatrakes and other folk healers in the inspired tradition, she would take no money for her services.[50]

Over the years I have met several people who have both practised and benefited from faith healing in a Christian context, and while these healing practices have come more to prominence with the reappearance of Charismatic Christianity in the twentieth century,[51] they nonetheless lie embedded in a folk tradition that goes back not only to Jesus Christ in the Gospels, but to Elijah, Elisha and other Old Testament prophets who performed healing miracles. I have encountered at first hand people who have enjoyed medically authenticated remissions from, or cures for, long-term debilitating arthritis, severe physical disability, and even breast cancer growths, in direct response to prayer.[52] This is, of course, an area where personal belief, medical assessment, the human body's own peculiar powers of recovery, and the miraculous all come together. It is, indeed, one of the most ancient therapies known, and has equivalents in other mainstream religious traditions as well as Christianity. And as a Christian myself, with a belief in a God who is active in the world and who responds to prayer, I have no difficulty in accepting the real existence of divine, miraculous healing, while being very much aware of the necessary safeguards that must be in place before we can certify a cure.

One of the most controversial and dangerous areas of faith healing in the late twentieth century, however, has been the active revival of a belief in demonic possession, as practised by certain Charismatic Christian groups. This approach to therapy, indeed, draws upon some of mankind's most archaic beliefs about the nature of illness that go back not only into pre-Hippocratic classical cultures, but even into prehistoric Shamanism. It was, and still is, most commonly invoked when dealing with certain aspects of mental illness, especially that of an hallucinatory or compulsive behaviour type.[53] Its obvious Gospel model lies in the account, narrated by St Mark, where Christ not only drives out, but even converses with, the demons expelled from the self-damaging lunatic Legion in the land of the Gadarenes.[54] And the same concept of possession was to manifest itself in many medieval heresy narratives and in the sixteenth-century 'witch craze', and was accepted as possible by John Wesley and by many Victorian spiritualists.

'Proper doctors' for everybody

A general access to reliable scientific medicine has been one of the most revolutionary features in the lives of most English people alive today. Whilst I have found many elderly respondents who retain fond loyalties to this or that herb or procedure, or take pride in 'getting themselves right', I have met none who did not show an awareness of the increased longevity and quality of life which modern medicine has made available to them. This has further been made possible by an easier access to the medical profession, and a decline in the god-like awe in which 'proper doctors' were once held by ordinary people.[55] Improvements in wages have also helped, for the average modern G.P. is likely to receive only three, four or five times the income of a skilled manual worker, rather than a differential of twenty or so times, as would have been the case in 1900.

Even so, the coming into being of a large class of people who must, for one reason or another, subsist on state benefits, or who are obliged to work for 'peanuts' wages, has only opened up another kind of social gulf during the 1980s and 1990s. And this modern form of poverty has brought its own medical problems, including heavy smoking, alcoholism, obesity, depression, and, *in extremis*, suicide. But people caught in this modern 'poverty trap' are at least more likely to be better informed than the poor of a century ago, and less likely to hold the medical profession, and 'the system', in such awe as to be afraid of seeking help when it is available.

L.S. Lowry, *The Doctor's Waiting Room* (1920). Here, Lowry – whose compositions are classic studies in human isolation of the poor of Salford and Manchester – very much captures the anxiety of an appointment with the doctor. (Salford Art Gallery.)

Along with the overall easing of financial and social gaps, moreover, the modern family doctor is less prone to treat his patient as an unlettered fool than he might once have been, which in turn leads to a greater and healthier mutual respect. Far from being rich men who employ debt collectors, most people, indeed, now think of doctors (and nurses) as martyrs to humanity, working all hours in an attempt to maintain a cash-starved National Health Service.

In these new conditions, the quack has become both an anachronism and an irrelevancy, though the case of the 1998 cancer-curer (see p.160) does indicate the resilience of quackery. Yet in spite of the advancing technical capacity of modern medicine, it is still a thing of no small wonder that practices on the fringes of scientific healing have come to enjoy a new lease of life in the twentieth century, in which many of the ancient priorities such as balance, purging, herbs and vital forces have taken on a new incarnation. This came about first with the rise of Naturopathy and Diet Reform

L.S. Lowry, *Ancoats Hospital Out Patients' Hall* (1952). Four years into the National Health Service, when scientific medicine was available to all, the pensive isolation of the patients seems just as great as before. (Whitworth Art Gallery, Manchester.)

among certain branches of the early twentieth-century middle classes, later developed a wider social agenda as alternative medicine, and by the 1990s became a form of healing that could work 'complementarily' with academic medicine in parts of the National Health Service.

6

Naturopathy, Diet Reform, and
the origins of alternative medicine

So far in this book my concern has been the popular, or
vernacular, medical traditions of the poor. Yet growing up in
the nineteenth century, and certainly by 1900, a more
prosperous middle-class tradition was emerging, especially in
Germany, Switzerland and America; a tradition, indeed, that
also sought relief from suffering outside or beyond the
ministrations of the formal medical profession, and this in
spite of its adherents' financial capacity to consult academic
doctors if they so wished. It emerged, in part, as a result of
the inability of academic medicine to cure a whole range of
diseases such as diabetes, cancer, depression, chronic
digestive disorders, degenerative conditions such as
arteriosclerosis, and 'wasting illnesses'. But perhaps more
importantly, it was fuelled by the consequences of changing
lifestyles in the wake of industrialisation. For just as
industrial workers were obliged by necessity to make do with
food of substandard nutritional value, so the wealthier
classes, who could afford to eat whatsoever they liked, were
becoming increasingly carnivorous. The cookery books of
the period show that the well-to-do ate meat three or four
times a day, and often in gargantuan quantities.

Industrial milling processes had supplied an abundance of
white flour (which all classes ate) which produced a stodgy
and less nutritious bread, while cheap refined white sugar
made artificially sweetened foods all the more commonplace.
Food, just like clothes and houses, has always been a badge of
social status; and the rapidly expanding middle classes of
Britain, France, and Germany – expanding thanks to the
burgeoning wealth of the London Stockmarket and the Paris
Bourse, especially during the 'railway mania' of the 1840s –
displayed their wealth in what they ate and what they did.

Too much meat, too many stodgy desserts, too much wine
and spirits and too much carriage- and train-riding began to

take their toll. And while many Victorian men could counterbalance this lifestyle by feats of prodigious walking (Charles Dickens regularly walked 12–15 miles a day after spending a long morning at his desk),[1] it was much more difficult for women. Corsets, voluminous skirts, multiple pregnancies and the social proprieties demanded that they live much more sedentary lives.

In consequence, the bourgeoisie not infrequently suffered from a complaint which they shared with their employees, and which could result from too much meat as well as from too much cheap stodge: constipation. It was pointed out in Chapter 1 that the Victorian working classes were martyrs to this complaint; but when it struck the better-off it could set off a whole train of consequences. A basically healthy, relatively inactive, constipated middle-class Victorian who was not faced with the necessary grind of earning his or her own living had the time to think dark thoughts. Allergies, melancholy, *ennui*, hypochondria and insomnia could generate a host of phantoms that contemporary physical and psychiatric medicine were powerless to handle, and which paved the way for a variety of possible curative responses.

This was in some degree to give rise to the *Lebensreform*, or Life Reform, movement in Germany, and the growing popularity of water cures, alcoholic temperance, and vegetarianism. England was the first country in the world to have a Vegetarian Society, in 1847,[2] based in Manchester; though German, French, American and Swiss equivalents followed. The early vegetarians argued that not only had chemical science shown that the substances found in vegetable carbohydrates were adequate for all processes of growth and vigour, but that meat was a form of nutritionally debased second-hand food that was left over after its original animal possessor had enjoyed the best of it. 'Dietetics', indeed, or the winning of health by diet and the reform of one's lifestyle, was the key.[3] Classical medicine was obviously looked back to by these people, for as we have seen, the gentle nurturing of the sick body back to health was a central feature of the agenda of Hippocrates and other ancient doctors. Similarly, the 'shock' therapies of contemporary Victorian academic pharmacy, in which drugs such as opium, mercury, bismuth, arsenic and antimony figured prominently, were castigated as loading the body with 'poisons'.

Now if a leisured, middle-class Victorian of the type mentioned above was obliged to consult a qualified physician about his constipation, tiredness, depression, or vague unwellness, he would invariably be subjected to a regimen of purges, calomel pills and other mineral drugs. Gradually sinking, and fearing the worst, he might be recommended by a friend to try Grafenburg Spa in Austria, or a new homeopathic practitioner whom the academic doctors labelled a 'quack', yet who was winning much attention. Or if it be as late as 1910, the unwell person might hear of a Swiss or American cure which invariably put one on top of the world after a 28-day fasting regimen with an abundance of water, fruit juice and vigorous exercise, in an early form of health farm. There the change of scene, plentiful exercise in the fresh air, absence of ingested metallic compounds, gallons of water, and enemas, would often work wonders, and the patient would return home a new man or woman. Yet once they gradually fell back into their old lifestyle, the familiar symptoms of depression, *ennui* and unwellness would return. After another bout with an academic physician, they might now choose to consult a fresh homeopathic healer or naturopath, or patronise a 'Sanatorium' or 'Health Home' that ran on 'new' principles. In short, there was a large market of vaguely unwell people with money in their pockets, in what was often called 'the pursuit of their health'.

Of course, it was not only the lifestyle and diet of the new urban middle classes which created the demand, but the inability of academic medicine to adequately cater for, or even take seriously, the sad as opposed to the mad, and the long-term vaguely unwell as opposed to the acutely sick. And what all these 'alternative' practitioners would give to their patients was an abundance of their time and a serious hearing, for that, after all, is what in part they were being paid for. Such a practitioner would never brusquely say to a patient 'pull yourself together' or 'stop moping', while going on to write out a prescription for a course of bismuth pills for the vague but worrying digestive disorder. On the contrary, the patient would be taken seriously, and given what we today would call a form of psychotherapy or counselling. It is not for nothing that the most successful naturopathic practitioners, then as now, have always been sympathetic, charismatic, or both.

Several therapeutic strands came together in the mid- and late nineteenth century to lay the foundations of what would become 'alternative' medicine. Mention has already been made in Chapter 4 of Vincenz Priesstnitz's water cures, and Dr Samuel Hahnemann's homeopathy.[4] Both of these movements, moreover, developed institutional bases in Europe and America well before 1900, with homeopathic dispensaries and private hospitals on the one hand, and imitative 'Grafenburgs' or 'Hydros' on the other. The famous 'Hydro' at Norbreck, for instance, high on the breeze-swept cliffs along the coast from Blackpool, Lancashire, used to pump its own supply of water from the adjacent Irish Sea, with which to douse and compress its patients.

In addition to hydrotherapy and homeopathy, the early decades of the twentieth century saw the rise of what was often called 'Diet Reform'. In this way of thinking, the old vague illnesses which nonetheless debilitated so many people were best prevented and cured by a fundamental change in what they ate. Certain aspects of this movement have a very modern ring to them, and in the latter part of the twentieth century came to have an impact on the eating habits of millions of people in the West who were not otherwise 'Diet Reformers': these included a preference for unrefined foods, roughage, green vegetables, an abundance of fresh fruit, and a ban on alcohol and tobacco. The prophet of Diet Reform in Europe was Dr Maximilian Oskar Bircher-Benner of Zurich, and in America John Harvey Kellogg, brother of the cereal manufacturer and head of the Seventh-Day Adventist Health Reform Institute at Battle Creek, Michigan.[5]

By 1910 both men, and their burgeoning number of disciples, were active on both sides of the Atlantic. That persistent enemy of good health – constipation and stomach trouble – would yield, it was argued, to fruit, oats, fasting, exercise and water. And with it would yield all the illnesses which the trapped-in poisons of constipation produced, such as cancer, depression, the seeds of consumption and diabetes, and all the symptoms of 'neurasthenia'. And just like Grafenburg and elsewhere, the new-style Swiss and American sanatoria actually worked for their patients – at least until the patients returned to a 'normal' lifestyle. But even so, they did have enduring effects on the eating habits of middle-class westerners, especially at the breakfast table, where Bircher-Benner's Swiss Müsli and Kellogg's Corn Flakes replaced the old morning orgies of meat and grease.[6]

All of these 'alternative' practitioners, from the self-taught Priesstnitz to the academically-trained Bircher-Benner (who was so concerned with not being dubbed a quack by his colleagues), were deeply classical in their concepts of health and medical practice, being Hippocratic even if they did not mention his name. Illness, for them, was caused by an obstruction to a 'vital process' which was best removed by the drug-free fast or internal irrigation. Then the body would be brought back into balance, and health somehow restored in default of infirmity.

While this approach to medical practice had – and still has – much to commend it, when dealing with people whose lifestyles and diets are punishing, its fatal flaw resides in its essentially simplistic concept of illness itself. Just as in Hippocrates, Dioscorides, Celsus, or any of the great classical writers on therapeutics, the body is seen as a naturally vigorous, self-righting, stable concourse of harmonious parts that needs only to be left alone to carry on to the end of eighty happy years. In this way of thinking, it is wrong foods, drinks, and practices that make us ill, as we erode our own natural vigour by bad habits.

Yet this 'alternative' approach to that of academic medicine failed to recognise the importance of systemic or degenerative diseases. Nor did it ever really recognise that living organisms are immensely complicated things, still imperfectly understood even by the finest physicians, and that complex diseases like cancer or mental illness can spring from a multiplicity of causes other than that of a sluggish colon.

D.S. Burton, of Harris, Pennsylvania, captured in the prime of manhood, before the practice of 'self-pollution' had asserted its grip over him. E.M. Ruddock, M.D. *et al.*, *Vitalogy: an Encyclopedia of Health and Home, Adapted for the Home, the Layman, and the Family* (Vitalogy Association, Chicago, 1930), p.863. (Author's collection.)

This is one of the main reasons why academic medicine had, and still has, its grave reservations about the rationale behind so much alternative medicine, especially when naturopathic healers purport to do battle with life-threatening conditions. Coming as the academic physician does, and has done for two centuries, from a view of the body as a combination of complex 'systems', any part of which can go wrong for a wide variety of still imperfectly understood reasons, it is not easy to take seriously the often apparently simplistic causes adduced by the naturopaths. It is even more difficult to do so when these simple causes are themselves

Mr Burton's haggard countenance after some three years' 'inveterate' practice of the 'self-polluting vice' of masturbation. Note the massive retouching of the photograph, almost qualifying it as a painting. It also seems from the shoulder line, jacket buttoning, and direction of light, that the faker reversed the original negative when printing the second photograph. Only the hairline and general posture belie its relationship to the original. E.M. Ruddock, M.D. *et al.*, *Vitalogy*, p.866. (Author's collection.)

pregnant with vagueness. Exactly which 'poisons' or 'toxins' cause which particular diseases, when no specific chemical compound or bacterium is ever mentioned? This was the direction from which the dreaded ridicule would come, when academically trained doctors like Hahnemann or Bircher-Benner were dubbed 'quacks' by their colleagues on account of their singular-cause pathologies. For while scientific physicians, even by 1900, were still impotent when it came to curing a wide range of diseases, they were at least making major inroads into understanding the disease process as a biological phenomenon, and even by this date had long since realised that it was an immensely complex process, and not likely to be beaten by simple solutions.

Dr Robert Bell and the medical case for vegetarianism

Yet one British advocate of vegetarianism and Diet Reform came from within the very heart of the Scottish medical establishment, and was a man who had no illusions about the complexity of the disease process. He was Dr Robert Bell, M.D., Senior Physician to the Glasgow Hospital for Women, and one of the foremost cancer specialists of his day, who turned down the offer of a baronetcy on the grounds of his relative poverty. By 1894 he had publicly renounced surgery as a treatment for breast cancer. On the one hand, he argued that in his experience about 50% of breast lumps turned out to be benign, so that surgery was wholly unnecessary. And sadly, surgery rarely ever seemed to cure actual cases of cancer, for the disease generally reappeared within three years and led to death.[7]

Bell began to look at patients' lifestyles as a way of understanding the pathology of cancer, and came to the conclusion, partly as a result of haematological studies – he was also the first medical scientist to take photomicrographs of pathological specimens – that cancer was generated in the blood. The blood came to be damaged, said Bell, by the eating of meat, especially in the excessive quantities that were fashionable in his day. A vegetarian diet, rich in cereals, fruit and vegetables, yet also containing nuts, cheese, eggs and milk, gave a person all the nutrition, salts and other substances necessary for good health. These foods, especially when eaten fresh and uncooked, prevented the constipation that often arose from a heavy meat diet, and avoided the 'autotoxaemia', or poisoning of the blood, through secretions in the gut.

At a time when metabolism and the body's immune system were scarcely understood, one can see how Bell's ideas were operating at the very edge of contemporary experimental medical knowledge when he spoke of the breakdown of a 'healthy metabolism' due to meat-product toxaemia in which the blood cells 'lose their normal power of resisting disease, which eventually will lead to their departing from physiological control'. It was after this defensive breakdown point that the body started to produce cancer cells.[8]

In his treatment of cancer patients after 1894, Bell developed a regimen of vegetarian dietetics, and in his published work claimed a high rate of success, especially in breast cancer reductions, without recourse to surgery. And as one of the first clinicians to recognise the difference between benign and malignant tumours of the breast, one wonders whether he was able to differentiate between the reduction of a malignant growth, and the natural diminution of a benign one.

In June 1912, Robert Bell was spectacularly vindicated in a lawsuit for libel, when he was awarded £2,000 damages and costs, against one Dr Bashford and the *British Medical Journal*, for calling him a 'quack'. Although still highly controversial, the quality and integrity of Bell's own research, and the testimony of many expert witnesses, showed that his non-surgical and dietetic approach to cancer could not simply be dismissed as eccentric.

It is hard, indeed, to overestimate the impact that a man like Bell had on the broader growth of the Life Reform movement in the early twentieth century. For here was a controversial physician of eminence, vindicated by law and a body of expert witnesses, who argued that dietetics could be the key to the cure of the 'greatest scourge' known to mankind – a scourge which Bell believed had already increased statistically several times over since his qualifying in 1868, and which he correlated with a recorded ten-fold increase of meat importation into Britain during the course of his professional life.[9] In the published newspaper account of his trial and vindication, it was pointed out that Galileo, Harvey and Lister had all been ridiculed in their time because of the apparently unconventional character of their discoveries, and one was left to put two and two together regarding Bell's work on vegetarian dietetics and cancer.[10]

The clientele of early alternative medicine

The rise of naturopathic or alternative approaches to medicine, as we have seen above, had nothing to do with the needs of the poor although, ironically, it did draw upon some of the same time-honoured classical precepts as those on which the Medicine of the People drew. But where, as we saw in the preceding chapter, the poor absorbed these precepts from a popularised vernacular tradition (to produce a chaotic armamentarium of practical precepts), the comfortably-off and no doubt better-educated disciples of Bircher-Benner and his colleagues were led by a diversity of self-conscious motives that could indeed stem from despair but were just as likely to spring from social ideology or Utopianism.

For one thing, early alternative medicine under its original titles of 'Naturopathy', 'Diet Reform', 'Life Reform', and such, was not especially a system of self-medication. Though it is true that individual people or households might administer their own medical or dietary regimens, its adherents generally operated in accordance with the teachings of a charismatic practitioner or writer. In short, it was what might be called 'guru-driven'. Unlike those sick persons who put themselves 'under' an academically trained physician, who practised in accordance with a set of internationally recognised scientific precepts, or the working-class person who practised *ad hoc* self-medication often in default of anything more affordable, the 'Life Reformer' adopted a therapeutic system or way of life that was in accordance with the precepts of a particular teacher, philosophy of health, or 'school'. Depending upon the teacher, therefore, one might have regular fasts, abstain from all meat or meat products, drink gallons of water, eat nothing other than fruit or only roughage-rich foods, take daily sunshine and air 'baths' in the garden, or do whatsoever one's chosen 'system' demanded to keep one's body forces in 'balance'.

And such an approach was by no means cheap. Quite apart from the cost of visiting a specialist sanatorium in Switzerland or elsewhere, the mere maintenance of a Diet Reform lifestyle required a serious outlay of time and money, and it is not for nothing that the pre-eminent British organ of the movement –

132

The 'Sun bath', seen by the early twentieth-century nature healers as a powerful therapeutic device. E.M. Ruddock, M.D. *et al.*, *Vitalogy: an Encyclopedia of Health and Home, Adapted for the Home, the Layman, and the Family* (Vitalogy Association, Chicago, 1930), p.830. (Author's collection.)

the periodical *Health for All* – possessed a clearly upper-middle-class tone. For one thing, the movement presupposed that its adherents had the time and the literacy needed to carefully study its publications. Furthermore, nutritionally adequate vegetarian foods, roughage-rich breads and flour, and large quantities of fresh fruit, were quite expensive and not easily available without the placing of special orders if one lived outside a major city. The new healthy breakfast cereal Shredded Wheat, for instance, was being advertised in 1927 at eighteen pence,[11] or one shilling and sixpence, per packet – a sum of money that could also have provided a hearty eggs, bread, jam and sweet tea breakfast for six people about to go off to a busy day in the factory!

The articles in *Health for All*, after its inception in 1927, and the related books and pamphlets issued by the company down to the 1950s, set the comfortably-off tone mentioned above. A conspicuous percentage of its writers and correspondents, for instance, had double-barrelled names, and there are occasional titled people, such as the surgeon Sir Arbuthnot Lane. They also used the occasional French or Latin word or phrase, and spoke of academically qualified doctors as members of the same social class, who really could not be relied upon not to 'poison' you.

The magazine *Health for All*, moreover, provides an informative window on to the British health movement by the 1930s. In addition to the main articles, it carried advertisements, with prices, for naturopathic foods and ingredients, details and terms for Diet Reform hotels and guest houses, and a monthly two-guinea prize for the patient who sent in the best essay account of overcoming a serious illness by fasting or related approved therapy. On the back cover of each number was a full-page, photographically illustrated advertisement for the 'Champneys' Health Home at Tring, Hertfordshire. Its Principal was the editor of *Health for All*, Stanley J. Lief, who was also an active public lecturer, journalist, and propagator of Diet Reform.[12]

It seems that one of the cornerstones of Lief's régime was the beneficent power of fasting, for anything up to 52 days. Stanley Lief had no claims to being the inventor of the long therapeutic fast, of course, for as F. Yeats-Brown emphasised, it had a classical lineage going back to the clinical practices of Hippocrates and Celsus, while all the great religious leaders – Christ, Mohammed, Zarathustra and Buddha – had fasted for long periods by way of spiritual and bodily discipline.[13] (Jesus Christ, for instance, fasted for 40 days and nights in the wilderness.) To the Latinate Yeats-Brown, indeed, the fast was the *vis medicatrix naturae* – the 'healing force of Nature'. And Lief was her latter-day prophet, especially in Britain, for the fasting cure, we are told, had long been 'popular' in America by 1927.

While by no means the initiator of the fast cure, therefore, Stanley Lief was its persuasive and charismatic evangelist in Britain, and his ministrations won him, amongst others, the discipleship of a clergyman, the Revd Walter Wynn, a hitherto medically orthodox university graduate who detested 'faddists', yet whom Lief relieved of a supposed 15-pound solidified mass of abdominal 'poisons', starting in December 1925. In the book describing his 52-day fast, the 59-year-old Wynn claimed that he had been given up by the doctors and told that his abdominal condition was inoperable. Though rather tantalisingly he gives no clinical name to his inoperable condition – the 15-pound mass of black poison seems to have been his own and Lief's graphic visualisation of it – one suspects that it was a malignant growth in the colon.[14]

Then the 14-stone-6-pound Wynn was put on a strict fast, though told to drink water every half-hour. Yet after four days spent dreaming of lamb chops, Wynn started to lose interest in food, began to shed a regular two pounds of body weight per day, and claimed to feel fitter and more mentally and physically active than he had been for years. As he only lived $1^{1}/_{2}$ miles away from 'Champneys', he became an outpatient, and soon found that he was virtually skipping the distance. He also preached and continued his Christian ministry each Sunday.

As the fast progressed, he was allowed a little nourishment by the sucking of the occasional orange, in addition to the constant draughts of water; and after a few weeks, Wynn was told by Lief that 'The hard mass of poison in the colon had been softening gradually. The water had bored holes in it. Water will soften and loosen a brick wall if you give it time.'[15] Indeed, Wynn became almost lyrical about the process, for 'The poison forced its way through my body in greater quantities than ever'; and one wonders whether he might have become temporarily 'high' from the prolonged absence of food. A sense of invincible well-being is not infrequently felt by those who fast.

Although, as was said above, the precise nature of Wynn's inoperable condition is never specified, his fast régime had sufficiently long-lasting consequences for him to still be penning enthusiastic booklets about water-cures and Sun and air baths three years later, when, at the age of 62, he could maintain a regular four miles per hour walking speed. He had clearly got better.[16]

Another hero of the 52-day fast was C.M. Trelawny Irving, who won the *Health for All* monthly prize for June 1927. Since 1919, indeed, Mr Trelawny Irving had suffered from constipation and other illnesses, and by 1925 was considering the surgical removal of his gall bladder.[17] Then he read a highly influential article on fasting by the American Upton Sinclair, originally published in the *Contemporary Review* in 1910,[18] and found new hope when he heard Stanley Lief lecture at Finsbury Park.[19] Trelawney Irving was converted to Diet Reform, took a 52-day fast, kept his gall bladder, and found his health. However, one suspects that there was something of a competitive element in long-term fasting, for the American fitness advocate Bernarr MacFadden wrote of 90-day fasts, in which 75 pounds of weight was lost.[20]

Indeed, the Prize Letters and other testimonial correspondence to *Health for All*, which seem fully authentic and uncontrived, do have an aspect of conversion about them which is almost reminiscent of religious 'witness' or 'conversion' literature. Like the sinner who finds the light, health-seekers usually speak of a sense of burden and dissatisfaction with life – which could have been due as much to *ennui* or depression as to an immediate physical cause – followed by a sense of catharsis and renovation. The water cure, the fast, or the new diet, unleashed energies that gave joy and a new purpose to life, and as none of these writers except the Revd Walter Wynn seem to mention the presence of a strong, independent religious motivation in their lives, one wonders how much the Holy Grail of 'finding one's health' also took upon it the mantle of a secular religion at a time when, in the neo-Darwinian 1920s and 1930s, many members of the educated middle classes were deserting traditional Christianity.

Other facts tended to strengthen the sense of brotherhood and sisterhood in Diet Reform, which further added to its 'religious' flavour. *Health for All* would sometimes contain a section entitled 'Champneys Chat. News from the Home of Health', in which Lief kept the faithful up to date with sanatorium news, almost as though it were a shrine which everyone was anxious to visit.[21] Diet Reformers, in their various forms, were also encouraged to bring up their children within the faith. A radiantly healthy-looking little Billy Lief is shown having a 'Sun bath' in the grounds of Champneys,[22] although one cannot help feeling sorry for the smiling little Mary Millwood, whose Diet Reform parents have brought up to have 'no milk puddings ... No tapioca ... No sweets and chocolate biscuits. No tea, coffee, or cocoa ... [and] no biscuits at school interval.' Mary's mid-day meal, moreover, was specified as containing 'no drink' (fluid, not alcohol) as this, presumably, would in some way upset her carefully worked-out diet.[23] One wonders if Mary Millwood's parents condemned traditional religious enthusiasts for having too many 'thou shalt nots' in their creed. It would be interesting to know what happened to her when she grew up.

Yet not all Diet Reformers who wrote about the bringing-up of children within the 'creed' were quite so prohibitory. The writings of Margaret Brady, M.Sc., have a refreshing vein of common sense running through them. She was even willing to allow white sugar, sweets and ice-cream in moderation. Her book *Children's Health* (1948) contains a section sensibly entitled 'A Warning Against Crankiness', in which she says: 'If the mother lets the diet become an end in itself it can very soon become a barrier to a better life rather than a key to it.'[24] Good health for the child, she says, is to 'intensify his sheer joy in living', and she deplored the psychological damage done to children by food-treat-forbidding parents.

Another aspect of Life and Diet Reform that displays a genuine pseudo-religious dimension is the cult of the body beautiful, or the body as a sort of temple of radiant energy. Some of the books and articles of Bernarr MacFadden, for instance, contain a narcissistic component, in which physical culture aims at a form of optimum health that appears to border on the self-obsessive.[25] The 1930s were the age when other aspects of physical culture, such as nudism, were also catching the headlines; and in Germany, organised physical culture was acquiring the shades of a full-blown pagan creed in Nazism. I am not suggesting that British physical culture and Life Reform had any such connotations in themselves, but the potential for human deification that was implicit within them could turn very nasty when encouraged by a vicious political régime.

The disease process as envisaged by early alternative medicine

When one reads through *Health for All*, the books which the company published and advertised, and the opinions which it espoused, one can piece together a full-scale alternative pathology or theory of disease, whereby illnesses are first thought to be generated, and the curative régimes are supposed to operate. Implicit in them all is the classical doctrine of balance, and the body's natural tendency to seek equipoise and health, in much the same way as a healthy plant will inevitably grow towards the light.

Within this pathology is the prevailing sense that we do not catch, or naturally develop, diseases, but that we somehow bring them upon ourselves. We do this by eating the wrong foods, eating the right foods in the wrong combinations, and, most of all, by eating so much that we leave the table feeling satisfied. Consequently, we develop constipation, build up lumps of poison – or, as Lief called it, toxaemia[26] – and are obliged to fast, and drink only water. Pleasurable eating becomes strongly redolent of sin and disobedience to the rules of health, and must be paid for by the penance of pain and fasting.

I am closely acquainted with four sisters, now in their late thirties and forties, who as children in the 1950s to 1970s were brought up on Diet Reform principles. They have told me how the quest for the ideal diet dominated their upbringing as children and adolescents, and how a superfluity of grated carrot, an overdose of vegetables and fruit in general, and an absence of meat, protein, and sometimes even carbohydrates, plus, at one stage, a weekly one-day fast, left them constantly preoccupied with food. One sister, when in her teens, used to

138

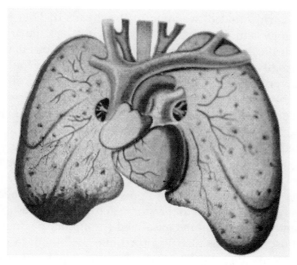

The lungs of Andrew Harper, an American who died 'from the Effects of Cigarette Smoking' about 1920. The early nature healers were among the first members of the medical community to highlight the dangers of nicotine poisoning. E.M. Ruddock, M.D. *et al.*, *Vitalogy: an Encyclopedia of Health and Home, Adapted for the Home, the Layman, and the Family* (Vitalogy Association, Chicago, 1930), facing p.848. (Author's collection.)

look longingly at the meat in butchers' shops: she could eat it raw, she said (she has since realised that she was suffering from severe anaemia at the time). Three of the four sisters subsequently developed anorexia, although admittedly other factors were also involved. The institution of this dietary régime had begun in an attempt to find a solution to the health problems of their father, who had a long history of stomach ulcers and undiagnosable bowel trouble. A friend had told him of Diet Reform, and he had spent time at Champneys in the late 1940s, during which his health had indeed improved, though this did not last. Thereafter the search for the 'perfect diet' ruled the family's culinary policy, as though once this were found, all problems would disappear. The main culprit in all the family's illnesses was thought to be 'catarrh', and the diets were aimed principally at its elimination.

'Catarrh', indeed, was one of the dreads of Diet Reform physiology and pathology. This was not just the irritating nasal stuff of colds, but was a universal evil mucus that could get virtually anywhere in the body to clog up and 'poison' it. It was very similar, indeed, to the classical humour, Phlegm. Inevitably, it was generated from wrong food.

Indeed, George R. Clements, who boasted the letters LL.B., M.D. after his name, had written on catarrh in 1928, and had rooted the condition mainly in meat products and in cakes, pies, bread and the like made with refined sugar and white, 'denaturalised', flour. The mischief inevitably began during digestion, when the 'poisonous gas' produced by unnatural fermentation in the stomach rose up the oesophagus to irritate and clog up the nasal and respiratory passages and the sinuses, and was also absorbed into the blood, to corrupt it! The only cure resided in a fast, to expel the poisons, followed thereafter by a strict diet.[27]

As catarrh in one form or another could cause anything from a bilious stomach, or even an ulcer, to tonsillitis, as well as general tiredness, it was clear that this universal culprit should be foreclosed upon at every turn. And this was done by a fast. A three-day fast could cure a cold, while George Clements claimed in 1928 to have cured a longstanding and debilitated victim of 'catarrh of the stomach and bowels' where the patient's weight dropped from 176 pounds to 124, and his skin took on a 'pink, healthy glow'.[28]

George Clements was an American who, before promoting the cause in Britain, was already a veteran of the nature cure in the United States, and had long been engaged in open warfare with the American medical profession and public health legislators. Clements' *The Villainy of Vaccination and Innoculation* (*c.*1927), which had received a conspicuous and approving notice in *Health for All* in November 1927, is, indeed, so 'over the top' in its ideas and language as to make the 'cranks' against whom Margaret Brady later warned look no more than mild eccentrics.[29]

One of the cornerstones of Clements' argument was a denial of the germ theory of disease – an opinion which he held along with one Dr E. Frazer in Canada, amongst others.[30]

Smallpox, in Clements' view, was not so much a killer disease as the product of a natural purge whereby the body expelled the poisons that were clogging it up. Even if germs existed, they were not the causal agents of disease, but rather the bystanders to a process whereby the body wrestled to evict its poisons, for health 'depends on the purity of the blood, the general tone of the organs, and the functional abilities of organs and fluids'. This doctrine lies at the centre of Clements' imprecise and highly generalised 'Law of Health'.

And then he goes on to make the amazing statement that 'Smallpox [is] a Beneficent Disease not to be Feared'. For just as the liver is always trying to purify the body, so the skin itself is a purifying organ, and smallpox is, in effect, a healthy body evacuation which takes place when the poisons reach a critical mass. Vaccination and innoculation were especially loathsome to Clements, and his book is redolent with terms like 'bovine filth' and 'putrid pus' when comtemplating the act of vaccination.

Like many nature healers, both in the 'educated audience' tradition and in the traditions of the poor, Clements was concerned with the absolute cause of a disease. Unlike the academic physicians – by whom disease is understood as a biological process that is identified symptomologically, and hopefully countered by a treatment devised in accordance with what is, as near as possible, a precise biological strategy – Clements villifies the physicians as charlatans and quacks because they do not know how diseases are generated *ex nihilo*. Sir William Osler[31] – one of the world's leading physicians up to his death in 1919 – is especially savaged on the grounds of his 'ignorance' for advocating vaccination while admitting that he does not know how smallpox is engendered from first principles. Clements then goes on to develop a full-scale conspiracy theory when he asserts that many members of the medical profession in both Britain and America do not accept the vaccination theory in their heart of hearts, but keep their doubts to themselves for fear of being struck off!

The basis of Clements' way of thinking, indeed, draws heavily on classical medical concepts: balance, blood, the

141

true causes of disease, the body as a sovereign, self-contained territory in danger of outside invasion in default of vigilance, and an almost obsessive concern with 'purity'. He even cites the Biblical Book of *Job*, to this end: 'Who can bring a clean thing out of an unclean? Not one', by which he means that health cannot be brought out of the animal 'filth' of smallpox vaccine which is developed from calves. Yet Clements' *pièce de resistance* of addled thinking, not to mention downright untruth, comes in his statement that 'death during smallpox never occurs under the management of drugless doctors, who understand that Natural Law is Universal.'[32]

Fantastic claims of the most dubious medical authenticity are by no means uncommon in the literature of naturopathic and early alternative medicine, however, for in addition to the familiar litany of cancer, tuberculosis, and other diseases being the result of constipation and ensuing poisoned blood, Benedict Lust, N.D., D.O., M.D., states categorically that 'Cancer develops very slowly ... from the thoroughly vitiated state of the blood and fluids'[33] (reminiscent, indeed, of the prior writings of Dr Robert Bell), and like consumption and smallpox 'can only be found in so-called civilised countries, and among people who are eating animal food.' Lust totally ignores the fact that completely vegetarian cultures are not very common outside the modern Western world, and that not only were cancer, tuberculosis and smallpox familiar to medical missionaries in all parts of the globe, but were also found in classical antiquity – being mentioned by the classical writers – and even in Egyptian mummy remains.

Harry Clements, D.O., seems from pictorial and other evidence in *Health for All* to have been the son of George, and carried on in the same tradition as his father, though one senses with less splenetic fury. In 1928, by which time he was practising as a naturopath in London,[34] Harry brought out a little book on the cure of appendicitis – a much-feared disease in the earlier part of the twentieth century – which stressed that operations were unnecessary, and that if one used the right diets and fasts, appendicitis would never occur in the first place.[35] Harry Clements, in fact (if it is indeed the same man), was still writing as late as 1978. His booklets on

Banishing Backache and *Diets to Help Prostate Troubles* still advise fasts, semi-fasts and diets to excise the universal bogey of constipation, for even in 1952 it 'is probably very difficult to find a person with a normal digestive tract'.[36] Indeed, everything from backache to appendicitis and prostatitis derived from a sluggish bowel.

Reading through the literature of the early twentieth-century naturopathy, Diet Reform, or Alternative Medicine movement, one is constantly struck by its selectivity. On the one hand, its continuing usage of blood, imbalance, cleansing and such place it within the tradition of Hippocrates. Conversely, however, its self-obsessive counter-culture aspects make it worthy of historical evaluation for a variety of reasons.

For one thing, its supposedly enlightened, literate middle-class devotees were not, one presumes, expected to notice certain fundamental incongruities in its doctrines. If, for instance, eating meat was not 'natural', and was a product of corrupt civilised living, why did human beings have incisor teeth and molars that were clearly designed for tearing and chewing flesh?[37] Why, moreover, was the human digestive tract not designed for cud-chewing like that of vegetarian animals, but for processing meat? Contemporary archaeological discoveries, furthermore, had shown that 'natural' man, living in the prehistoric cave or in a part of the world as yet untouched by 'civilisation', was an omnivore, and willing to eat meat, fruit, or whatever the environment provided. And why, since the first 'pus puncher', Dr Edward Jenner, had introduced vaccination in 1798, had the life expectancy at birth of a British man or woman risen from below 40 to 63 years?[38] All of this information, indeed, was easily available in any public library by 1925.

The movement was not without its genuine insights, however, for it not only gave us modern breakfast cereals, but also a growing awareness of the importance to health of wholemeal flour products, fresh vegetables and fruit, and of the desirability of eating more moderately-sized meals. And in its historical alliance with temperance and anti-smoking movements, naturopathic medicine undoubtedly drew attention to commonly injested substances that were truly dangerous long before things like anti-smoking campaigns became part of official medical and social policy.

Yet one aspect of this movement which I believe made it very much of the middle classes and which separated it from the more eclectic medicine of the poor was its very systematic or 'secular religion' tendencies. For in many respects the twentieth-century naturopathic and dietetic precepts discussed in the present chapter had a relatively limited impact on the broader sweep of the Medicine of the People as considered elsewhere in this book. For one thing, middle-class naturopathy was too expensive and too time-consuming for most working people. It also depended too much on elaborately thought out and executed 'systems', and there was too much pedagogical dependence upon the teachings of charismatic gurus like Stanley Lief. Working people, after all, were already bossed about by too many people – employers, council officials, rent collectors, and Public Assistance Inspectors – to also want to have their dinner tables policed.

But the biggest single disadvantage which dietetics possessed for poor people was its spectacular dullness and joylessness. In its sanctimonious 'noes' to everything pleasant or tasty, it embodied some of the most detested traits of killjoy puritanism. As George Orwell summed up the Diet Reform movement with relation to the ill-nourished inhabitants of Wigan in 1937: 'The ordinary human being would sooner starve than live on brown bread and raw carrots... A millionaire may enjoy breakfasting on orange juice and Ryvita biscuits: an unemployed man doesn't.'[39] Indeed, the sight of 'bad' foods such as bully-beef, chips, white bread and butter, jam, sugar, beer and sweet tea might induce neurasthenic fibrillations in a regular visitor to the Champneys Health Home; but they gave joy to the hard life of a coal miner. One also suspects that heroic fasting régimes had less appeal to people who could not, like the Revd Walter Wynn, 'pass through the dining-room of the Savoy Hotel at luncheon time',[40] and who had an all too familiar sense of hunger that was engendered by inadequate wages and periodic bouts of unemployment.

On the other hand, it should not be forgotten that even during the late Victorian period vegetarianism had its working-class devotees. In April 1888, for instance, Thomas Mansell, foreman at the Thames Ironworks in London, travelled up to the Brotherton Hall, Manchester, to address the Vegetarian Society on 'Vegetarianism and Manual Labour'. Mansell claimed that he and his wife had been healthy vegetarians for thirteen years, and that both his indigestion and his wife's varicose veins, along with a serious but unspecified illness, had been cured by vegetarianism. He also claimed to be acquainted with other heavy manual workers who were also vegetarians, in spite of the popular belief among the working classes that meat gave you strength. Then Mansell adds a comment reminiscent of a 'conversion' account, when he says to his (middle-class) vegetarian audience that within the working class 'many are gradually coming to our side'.[41] I have, however, found very little reference to vegetarianism amongst my own elderly respondents.

Ironic though it may seem, I would argue that the medicine of the poor was much more scientific in its approach than was naturopathy; for like academic medicine, it was governed by practice and by experimental results, rather than by philosophical rules or social ideologies. For rules, abstract principles, and philosophies of life mattered far less than did the curing of the immediate pain. And if working-class people became ill, they would, by necessity, try whatever was available to 'right themselves' again. This could mean a visit to the corner shop for a box of Beecham's Pills, to the herbalist for a 'Sulphur Tonic', to a friend's allotment to collect enough rhubarb to 'shift heaven and earth', or to a 'proper doctor' to seek hospital admission if they felt sufficiently 'far gone'.

How much of dietetics, naturopathy, and sanatorium culture actually survived to become part of late-twentieth-century alternative medicine was by transforming themselves into the Health Farm and its extramural adjuncts. Still catering for a well-to-do clientele wanting emotional comfort and reassurance, the early-twentieth-century Health Home had to rethink its strategy if it was to stay in business. By the

1960s and 1970s there was a whole class of persons who had once formed a staple component of the clientele of Health Homes like Champneys, and yet who were no longer in the market. For in addition to the round of sluggish bowel victims and dietary puritans, the 1930s still saw large numbers of people who were struggling against clinically defined yet largely incurable illnesses. These included people with systemic tubercular disorders, deteriorating diabetic complications, and gastric ulcers, and a whole host of individuals who suffered from manic depression, schizophrenia, and other conditions which were sufficiently troublesome to make life a misery, yet not bad enough to require formal or long-stay hospitalisation. Where had they gone?

It is my argument that by the third quarter of the twentieth century a number of the 'filthy poisons' that orthodox medical research was actively developing were beginning to scythe through many of these chronic conditions. Streptomycin-based antibiotics had largely consigned tuberculosis to the dark ages in the West by 1960, while Lithium, Largactil and other psycho-active drugs were changing the entire management of depressive diseases by removing anxiety awareness and enabling many mentally ill people to find more peace, joy and fulfilment in life than they ever could have imagined in 1930. Similarly, major progress had been made in the management of gastric ulcers. The increasing mass-production of insulin at the same time was transforming the lives of diabetics. And after the founding of the National Health Service in 1948, it was a point of explicit political and social policy that these and future 'wonder drugs' should be available to all, and be paid for out of taxation.

With this large catchment of the chronically-unwell so much diminished, and the post-1948 situation where, suddenly, free National Health Service treatment was medically every bit as good as that which one could obtain in an exclusive private clinic, institutional naturopathy had to rethink its rôle or face financial disaster. What took place, in fact, was a subtle yet decisive change of emphasis. The new Health Farms did not purport to cure illnesses by their particular régimes, but to make people feel better within and about themselves. With that explosion of prosperity which came with the 'You've never had it so good' decade that began in the mid-1950s, moreover, new social pressures were created that gave rise to a new type of well-off fee-paying clientele which was a world removed from the constipated colonels, dyspeptic maiden aunts and depressed debutantes of the 1920s and 1930s. Now there were the rock stars, film stars, sports personalities and popular entertainers, the over-stressed businessmen, the media personalities, and those whose marriages had been damaged by their partner's meteoric success, and who now felt unloved and inadequate. Growing media pressure, especially on women, further created an obsession with 'perfection': a perfect figure, a perfect career, a perfect marriage, and a perfect sex-life. Detoxification was still strong, however, but was now usually aimed at treating conditions induced by tobacco, alcohol, or recreational drug abuse. 'Feel-good' spartan diets were designed to relieve the obese of their stones and pounds, while the politically correct 'colonic irrigation' or 'colonic hydrotherapy' replaced the old-fashioned enema. On the whole, however, these farms and clinics were not supposed to be curative, but rather wellness-inducing institutions: a subtle, yet legally vital, shift of emphasis. Like so much modern alternative medicine, in fact, they wisely moved away from healing in any precise clinical sense, and concentrated more upon making the client feel good. Balances were to be restored, anxieties mollified, 'stress levels' reduced, Yin and Yang harmonised, and 'wholeness' restored.

This is the direction, indeed, in which alternative medicine developed during the last forty years of the twentieth century: to cater for needs which neither the original Diet Reform Health Homes of the wealthy nor the indigenous Medicine of the People could ever have envisaged in the inter-war period.

These needs in themselves, moreover, are also reflections of the rapidly changing society which grew up in Britain after World War II. For while the broadly socialist culture of the post-1945 era produced the scientific paternalism of the National Health Service, the swing towards a market-driven culture after 1980 enshrined at its heart the individual's right to choose. In many respects, this market culture was anti-authoritarian, and assumed that one had the right to choose not only one's lifestyle and spiritual beliefs, but also one's approach to medicine. Wellness could be sought, therefore, in homeopathy, crystal therapy, reflexology, aromatherapy, or in what, even by 1984, added up to a list of 73 systems of alternative or complementary therapies.[42]

And as mentioned at the end of Chapter 5, modern doctors, especially of the younger generation, came to reflect these social changes in their relations with their patients. For while G.P., surgery, and hospital time was always on a tight budget, many modern doctors, just like the old-time quacks or naturopathic healers, came to understand that a patient's feelings, preferences and dislikes had to be brought into the equation if the healing process was to be effective. In consequence, a substantial minority of G.P.s came to realise that certain therapeutic systems dear to the philosophy of life of the individual patient might with profit be incorporated into the broader healing package, to 'complement' their scientific medicine. And if this genuinely helped the patient to get better, then all well and good; for as I have emphasised on several occasions, scientific medicine is a practical, experimental activity, the first priority of which is to save and improve lives.

So naturopathy, alternative medicine, and then complementary medicine have found places for themselves in the world of efficacious scientific medicine, and have shown that the Medicine of the People is indeed a tenacious survivor.

7

A tenacious survival:
the classical tradition today

The Medicine of the People, especially as traditionally practised by the poor, has by its very nature never been at the forefront of its time, and excepting any influences from the naturopathic movement, always existed as a cultural hand-me-down. On the other hand, it has always had a surprisingly versatile way of looking at health, capable of absorbing anything which was found to be useful without undermining its basic assumptions. It became, in short, a supremely practical creation aimed not at solving intellectual problems, but at gaining useful results. Just as it was capable of absorbing the practical or explanatory elements of classical Greek medicine in the days of the Tudors, and homeopathy in the days of Victoria, so it adopts and adapts today. This often results in people carrying around with them a diverse armamentarium of ancient and modern medical beliefs, each of which can be drawn upon as the particular circumstance requires. We still fall in love with our hearts (in accordance with the physiology of Aristotle), while at the same time finding no incongruity in surgically transplanting the same organ. Likewise, our blood 'boils' when we are angry, though in our saner moments we know that if its temperature were to rise much beyond $98°.4$ F we would die. This is, moreover, a multi-level medical awareness which is in no way restricted to the elderly, but continues to be passed on to the enthusiastic young. A Manchester G.P. related to me an excellent example of a young mother of about twenty-four who brought her child to be examined. She summed up both disease and imagined cure by stating: 'Doctor, Little Willy has got hot blood. I think that he needs an antibiotic.'[1]

Many factors contribute to keeping this culture alive, one of which is the medical profession itself. Several doctors have told me that when explaining the grounds for a particular course of medication to a patient, they will, for simplicity's sake, describe it in a language which the person will understand. This is particularly true for elderly patients being treated for circulatory complaints. One St Bartholomew's Hospital physician told me that when prescribing medication to elderly patients, he will say that they need something to 'thin down' their blood, for this graphic analogy will conform to expectations and thereby ensure that the pills are taken.[2] Many elderly people themselves have told me that their doctors have prescribed blood pressure tablets to thin down their blood, and in a way this is what they do. Medicines administered to regulate a defective heart action will sometimes be nicknamed 'gunpowder' tablets, from the way in which they are supposed to provide extra power to the organ. Doctors will also use local or dialect words to help a patient better understand their complaint, and I believe that the Liverpool area forms an interesting melting-pot of such terms, where Lancashire, Welsh and Irish words converge.[3] If the medical profession is willing, only occasionally, to speak thus to its patients, it is hardly to be wondered that the tradition survives.

Likewise, modern 'alternative' medicine and related movements which grew up in the wake of twentieth-century naturopathy often draw deeply on ancient folk ways in their thinking. It is of some interest, moreover, that the great majority of adherents to modern alternative medical movements are not the Edwardian survivors but their grand- and great-grand-children. Most elderly people, indeed, are firm supporters of scientific medicine, to which they rightly attribute their increased health and longevity. Many active eighty-odd-year-olds have told me that their own parents were dead before fifty, or of beloved relatives who were swept away by 'the consumption'. As we saw in Chapter 6, modern drugs might be 'poisons', but they can destroy diseases as well as humans, and the great generality of elderly people are unanimous in their appreciation of the life-saving power of scientific medicine, made accessible through National Insurance and the National Health Service, and dread its possible dismantling by cost-cutting politicians. Yet an increasing number of physicians in the N.H.S. are also willing to work in tandem with some of the patients' preferred natural therapies, as a way of complementing the scientific medicine, if it is likely to hasten the healing process.

It is an irony of our time, however, that the elderly who were often brought up on herbs and *Aristotle's Works* should now so firmly swear by their tablets, while their great-grand-daughters claim a right to 'natural' childbirth and preservative-free wholefoods. But this popular return to folk ways would not have been possible in a society where scientific medicine was not constantly advancing, and not instantly available to step in when the folk ways proved inadequate.

'Alternative' or 'complementary' medicine continues to characterise both itself and its remedies as 'natural', while still envisaging nature as a goddess abused by scientists. A natural medicine is generally thought of as something in its raw or uncontaminated state, as opposed to something artificial, or the product of human invention. What alternative medicine often fails to appreciate, however, is that so-called simple substances in nature are often highly complex and unpredictable in their action, whereas those 'artificial' ones administered by the doctor are pure and more likely to be singular. If one speaks of the poppy plant, for instance, one might imagine relieving pain 'naturally' by means of a botanical juice. Yet in reality this juice of the poppy is one of the most complex alkaloid groups known to chemistry, with around forty active substances in it. If a person is injected with morphine, he or she is receiving a pure extracted form of the poppy alkaloid which is one of the best pain-killers known to medicine. Heroin, another major pain-killer, is a compound related to the same poppy juice. Yet it is absurd to think of the complex and chemically unpredictable juice of the raw poppy as more beneficial than a precisely measured dose of one of its pure active ingredients. The same applies to virtually all plant and herbal substances. This belief in the greater reliability of simple vegetable (as opposed to mineral) substances leads, in turn, to one of the central precepts common to certain schools of twentieth-century alternative medicine; namely, that drugs (and what my grandmother called 'chemics') are bad, and poison the body.

A related precept from the old tradition to survive into modern alternative medicine is a confirmed preference for self-medication. 'Nature's way' is not to be found in the physician's consulting room, and if experts are to be countenanced at all, then they should be practitioners of a folk tradition, who speak a language which their clients understand. Herbalists, homeopaths and naturopaths have not only maintained a tenacious hold, but, aided by shrewd marketing and advertising, have turned themselves into components of a major international business. And a major way in which they have done this has been through adapting to new market demands.

Many businesses have been founded, over the last decade or so, on the smart selling of natural products, one of the most successful of which is Culpeper the Herbalist.[4] This firm, which opened many branches in southern England in the 1980s, attempted to create the ambience of the old herb shop, packing its small, cosy premises with numerous bottles, jars and cabinets, while loading the air with rich and fragrant botanical aromas. Though some herbal medicines are sold, a large part of the market is the retail of herbal hair and skin lotions along with cosmetics. Whenever I have visited a Culpeper shop, however, I have been struck by the relative youth of the clientele, for instead of old ladies looking for bunches of herbs, one is more likely to encounter young ones looking for 'natural' toiletries. It says much about the packaging of a natural health business, that such a commercial success can be based on the name and reputation of a seventeenth-century botanical writer and astrologer (a framed portrait of whom hangs in each branch) who was ridiculed even by the scientific practitioners of the 1670s. Modernised editions of Culpeper's *Compleat English Physician* and *English Midwife* (now the *Book of Birth*) are also on sale, though omitting the original astrological content.

Indeed, one significant feature of most 'natural health' and self-medication shops today is that they rarely sell products which claim to cure diseases. The stress is much more on soothing, cleansing and invigorating. The implication is that one should gently aid the body, avoid those poisons which prevent imbalance, and frustrate the conditions from which diseases spring. In an age when most people are likely to apply to a scientifically trained doctor when gripped with serious illness (and in which one is restrained by law from advertising cures for many diseases), this is the sensible strategy for the commercial alternative healer. Natural medicine, therefore, ceases to be a cure, and instead becomes a general philosophy of health, grounded in prevention and a homely fondness for 'simple' products. When substances purporting to be medicines are sold, it is more likely that they are aimed at vague, non-lethal classes of ailments and are homeopathically related.

In addition to the chains of fashionable 'olde worlde' health shops, there are many smaller independent concerns across the country which sell a wide range of health products, extending from home brewing kits to homeopathic preparations. Some years ago I had an interesting conversation with the manager in charge of one of these shops in the Manchester area. She placed great stress on self-medication, though not denying the importance of doctors for serious illnesses. She tended to imply, rather, that doctors would hardly be necessary if people followed nature's way, avoided poisons, drank plenty of water and ate a balanced diet. Ironically, what she said sounded very similar to what Stanley J. Lief predicted for 'The Doctor of To-morrow' in 1928, when 'a real physician (teacher) could intelligently advise you how to harmonise your living with Nature's Immutable Laws'.[5] There is, of course, a great deal to commend in this approach, and its common sense can be generally acknowledged, so long as we remember that diseases in most cases are not simple things, amenable to simple cures.

On the other hand, the manager in the Manchester health shop argued, as a homeopath, that not only were many diseases caused by poison and imbalances, but that the patent manufactured homeopathic remedies on sale in her shop were the best cures for most common complaints. Like my elderly respondents, she spoke of health as similar to gardening, insofar as she thought of the healing process as a gentle nurturing of the body. Modern medicine was too drastic in its approach, as well as too drug-based. In short, she expressed a tradition which very much encapsulates the one so far described in this book, with its stress on blood, balance and cleansing. This lady also gave me several homeopathic leaflets, dealing with what seemed to be a series of fairly broad ailments, such as backache, women's problems and children's diseases. For all of these disorders, there was a simple homeopathic solution, based on the administration of attenuated doses of simple salts aimed at correcting an imbalance in the body. She informed me that more leaflets were in the course of production, and that there was a very thriving custom for the medicines. As a course of homeopathic medicines would have worked out more expensive than the charges for a National Health prescription, one wonders at the source of their appeal. Most likely, it is rooted in the very deep desire of every man and woman to be their own doctor.[6]

During the twentieth century, alternative medicine has shown a clear tendency to move up-market, far away from its once plebeian roots. This not only applies to health farms and to elegant herb shops in city-centre locations, but also to the character of its advertising. Some years ago the actress and television personality, Katie Boyle, lent her well-preserved good looks and fitness to a firm of homeopathic preparation manufacturers. 'Thank goodness for Nelson's homeopathic remedies', said the posters featuring Miss Boyle; while one notes that the firm manufactures homeopathic remedies and not medicines.[7]

The up-market ambience is also maintained by many alternative, homeopathic and natural healers, who set up consulting rooms and fashionable practices. While resort to such practitioners can hardly be classed as self-medication, one must bear in mind that it is much more in keeping with traditional folk practices, where the advice of the naturopath or herbalist is sought rather than that of the orthodox physician.

Many of the people who resort to these practitioners are far from old (as are the people who patronise herb shops), and one north Manchester friend told me of such a consultation which she made in 1987. Advice about a persistent, tickling cough had been sought from a naturopathic healer practising in Fleetwood, Lancashire. The practitioner was well-dressed, operated from a set of elegantly furnished consulting rooms, and was wholly professional in his manner.

Concluding his diagnosis, he informed the patient that the seat of her cough was the liver, which was not functioning properly and was emitting a substance which irritated her throat. Although he advocated multivitamins, the central feature of his prescribed cure lay in the taking of three herbs, three times per day. The herbs were cumfrey, Devil's claw and sasparilla, compounded together in tablet form, and were to be taken for exactly eighty-four days, which is the duration of three lunar months. The lady was also put on a diet excluding red meat, and told that at the expiry of the eighty-four days, not only would her liver have been rectified to cure her cough, but her eyes would have been strengthened by way of a bonus, enabling her to discard her spectacles.

Although his manner and presentation was quite different, I could not help feeling that there were several parallels here to Mr Bigwood, the Corsham 'Licensed Botanist' of 1875, discussed in Chapter 5. Mr Bigwood, it will be recalled, had also located a cough (in his case, a consumptive one) in the liver, and treated it with a numerologically significant collection of herbs in a precise astrological context. The modern Lancashire practitioner skilfully used many of the traditional components of folk medicine, with his stress on liver, blood, poisons, herbs and hierarchies, but now re-marketed via a business suit and consulting rooms. Adopt, and adapt, and you need never perish.

In the *Yellow Pages* for north Manchester in 1987 there were more than fifty listed health and wholefood shops, eight herbalists, four homeopaths, and one naturopathic clinic. By 1998–9 these had grown to such an extent that the same *Yellow Pages* classified 'Complementary Medicine' and 'Complementary Therapies' under no less than fifteen separate specialist headings, to guide people inquiring into shops, practitioners, or clinics for homeopathy, reflexology, acupuncture, and so on, to the appropriate entries.

One other aspect of traditional medicine which has made a recent, if brief, reappearance is the retributive, or divine punishment, theory of disease. Just as John Wesley was willing to countenance that many diseases stemmed from human wickedness, and some modern Charismatic Christians believe that mental illness is a product of demonic punishment, so the AIDS epidemic in its early days elicited a similar response in some quarters. God can chastise with a 'gay plague' in the same way as earlier ages saw Him sending syphilis or the sweating sickness. Though it is true that this theory rapidly lost its appeal when AIDS ceased to be seen as an exclusively homosexual affliction, it still shows how ancestral ways of looking at disease can remain close to the surface.

Although this study has largely been concerned with the survival of ancient medical ideas in northern England, there is no reason to assume that it is a uniquely English, let alone a northern English, phenomenon. The precepts of ancient medicine provide the conceptual framework of several Californian health cults which 1 have encountered, and there is evidence of its survival elsewhere in the United States and Latin America. Many parts of North America, such as the Appalachian region and the Midwest, were settled by the poor of England and Europe between the seventeenth and nineteenth centuries, and it is hardly surprising that they took the Medicine of the People with them.[8] Homeopathy also enjoyed great popularity in late nineteenth-century America, while in the Minnesota region I have found fragments of popular classical and homeopathic medicine engrafted on to a local Indian medical tradition.[9] Jamaica and the English-speaking Caribbean also has its own eclectic medical traditions, in which pieces of antiquated European medicine coalesce with those of Africa. Though it is not an area which I have researched specifically, I understand that many West Indian people in England today preserve an indigenous medical tradition which draws in part on humoral and related explanations. The same applies to the ethnic medicine of the Asian communities in Britain, and Dr Mohammed Aslam's study in the 1970s has shown how the practice of Hakim medicine, with its classical concepts of balance, heat, and humours, could be found in modern Britain.[10] I am not, however, aware of the extent, if at all, to which Hakim medicine has spread from British Asian communities to join the wider stream of alternative medicine.

One form of ancient non-European medicine which has been taken up keenly by Western people is that of China. Traditional Chinese medicine in its various forms has acquired a remarkable following; and acupuncture especially, with its concept of body 'meridians' or lines of life and power, has come to be extensively practised. While acupuncture – consisting as it does of the insertion of fine needles into specific locations in the body's 'meridians' – is an expert rather than a self-help system of medicine, it has become very popular. And in addition to its proven capacity to control pain, it has been called upon to treat a wide array of rather unspecific yet genuinely troublesome conditions, such as stress, tension, and tobacco addiction.

While ginseng has been around for years as a universal cure-all, during the 1990s many English towns acquired Traditional Chinese Medicine shops, where one can buy roots, barks and various other preparations with which to self-medicate, or be advised upon a wide range of maladies. Yet traditional Chinese medicine is very similar in its conceptual basis to that of the West. Like the therapeutics of Hippocrates, Chinese medicine is about the putting of the body back into balance, which it tries to do by the stabilisation of Yin and Yang, which represent the opposites of female and male, cold and hot, down and up, and so on. Unlike the New Age forms of alternative medicine (which will be discussed below) Chinese medicine is not occult or mysterious, and stands to some degree on the same empirical basis of tried and trusted herbal substances as does that of ancient Greece.

The 1990s also saw the extensive popularisation of several new forms of alternative medicine, such as aromatherapy and crystal therapy. While the erotic powers of perfumes and the repellent powers of foul stinks have been understood from time immemorial, and the ancient Romans used crystal amulets for a wide variety of purposes – amethyst, for instance, was supposedly a cure for hangover – one suspects that the development of these ways of thinking in our own time owes a great deal to the rise of New Age cults. By the late 1990s, moreover, virtually every town of any size in Britain had a 'New Age' shop which purported to sell crystals, amulets, or other artefacts which would 'focus earth powers' for their possessor. While not daring to claim that these 'powers' can cure cancer or schizophrenia, for instance, they are nonetheless supposed to conduce to 'wholeness', help one to stop smoking, or improve one's love life.

It is interesting to notice how, in addition to alternative medicine's general tendency towards self-help, the growing trend towards 'holistic' healing has placed an increasing emphasis upon the spiritual dimension of being well. This, in turn, has paved the way for experts and teachers above and beyond the 'gurus' of the Health Reform movement of the 1920s. Summoning up healing 'powers' from the earth, from God, or from within the individual person undergoing treatment has become important in modern non-scientific healing, and one of its most remarkable manifestations has been the growth of the healing ministry in modern-day Charismatic Christianity (mentioned in Chapter 5) which claims to draw upon the same divine force whereby Christ and his disciples healed the stricken.

And most of the strands within the modern-day Medicine of the People have their magazines and literature. On the whole, however, the tone of these publications is very different both from that of the writings of the Victorian quacks who tried to sell their nostrums to the poor, and also from that of the Diet Reform literature of the 1920s and 1930s. Modern health literature contains no threats. No one will die if they fail to buy a particular preparation, and readers are not being extolled the virtues of seven-week fasts; though it is true that some slimming magazines can be more strict when it comes to that particular form of self-discipline. On the whole, however, modern health magazines are bright and cheery publications, not being that much removed from other (usually women's) magazines that have substantial sections on various aspects of health and against which they must compete on the newsagents' stands.

Here's Health – the successor to *Health for All* – for instance, is positive and up-market in its tone, aiming at a young and probably female readership, and is a world removed from its somewhat grim and authoritarian ancestor of seventy-odd years ago. Instead of the old articles on fasting and minimalist eating to help the long-term unwell, it now sets out to explain the various alternative therapies, provides menus for modern healthy eating (as opposed to starving), advises healthy women about the menopause, has feature interviews with leading nature healers, and discusses psychological well-being. It accepts the claims and powers of modern medicine, recommends vitamins, hormonal treatments and the like, and yet suggests that aromatherapy, reflexology and an holistic lifestyle can make major contributions to keeping one feeling young and fit. In short, contemporary alternative medicine, as suggested above, is no longer for the seriously ill, but for the healthy. Yet in so many ways this is exactly the original nature of the classical medical tradition, as the ancient 'regimens' of health and their medieval, Tudor and Georgian successors strove to keep the humours in balance so that the predator of disease could not even obtain a foothold.

When one considers the way in which popular medicine grew over the course of centuries, and the intuitive knack which it developed for working with whatever useful procedures came to hand, it is hardly surprising that it has come to take modern scientific medicine in its stride. Like a living language, a living medical tradition learns to operate on many different levels. Though originally the product of poverty and the preserve of those who could afford no better and mistrusted social superiors, it developed a great versatility rooted in common sense and a keen power of observation. It is no wonder, therefore, that when scientific medicine suddenly became both efficient and easily available in the middle of the twentieth century, the popular tradition was not destroyed but came to absorb it.

As soon as people could come to depend on scientific medicine to live longer and healthier lives, folk medicine could cease to be a survival tool and become a form of hobby or lifestyle. As such, it could incorporate the accumulated wisdom of past generations without having to rely upon its effectiveness in time of crisis. As such, it could also pave the way to the revival of herbalism, homeopathy, and night-school classes in 'nature's way'.

Nor must we forget that in this market-place of therapeutic choices, bare-faced, old-fashioned quackery still raises its head from time to time, though its exponents increasingly run the risk of incurring a legal penalty. As recently as January 1998, for instance, at Wigan, Lancashire, magistrates passed sentence upon a local man who had a national 'chain selling operation' for the retail of colloid of silver that could allegedly treat an incredible 650 diseases, including cancer and AIDS. A month's supply of this simple solution sold for £22.95, and was condemned by an expert witness cancer specialist as giving 'false hope to sufferers'.[11]

In conclusion, one must ask: how effective is natural medicine? Responses tend to be varied, depending largely upon how seriously one expects a cure and of what type, while at the same time realising that one is only likely to be using such therapies for minor aches and pains or beauty treatment rather than for serious illnesses. I have encountered many people who have assured me that their eczema, headache or stiff joints were eased – at least temporarily – by this or that herb, and one has no need to doubt their claims. Many herbs *do* possess genuine healing powers, and so long as one maintains priorities and does not try to tackle cancer, schizophrenia, or diabetes, they can do good.

Homeopathy likewise has its firm adherents. Many people who regularly take homeopathic remedies have reminded me that Her Majesty the Queen is an adherent, and one cannot deny that the loyalty of prominent persons to particular therapies bestows a certain authority upon them. The resort of other sometime members of the Royal Family – such as the late Princess Diana, and the Duchess of York — to spiritual and natural healers only confirms the seriousness of the 'alternative' option to many people. At a less exalted level, people also tend to be impressed when a pop singer or actress gives a press interview in which their preference for drug-free or natural cures is mentioned. Indeed, when one contemplates the West End homeopath, ministering to a fashionable clientele of pop stars, one appreciates how tenacious the ancient tradition can be, and how far it has moved up market. And on a more mundane level, the ordinary person loyal to their seaweed pills or homeopathic 'kali phos' (potassium phosphate) can take many minor burdens off the shoulders of the National Health Service, and can play a serious role in maintaining their own sense of wellness.

The modern natural health movement also performs an invaluable service in its condemnation of smoking, heavy drinking, drug-taking and bad diet – a condemnation, indeed, that goes back to the earliest days of naturopathic medical practice, and still constitutes one of its most valuable and enduring services to modern health. For the sensible modern person is encouraged to eat and drink more wisely than ever before, while the excessive use of stimulants is uniformly deprecated by both naturopathic and orthodox scientific healers. In this respect, alternative medicine forms an important ally to the scientific, thereby truly complementing it, in stressing the need for a less polluted world. Yet the fact must not be missed that natural medicine, in whatever form, is ultimately a refinement to a fundamental health standard, and is only practically feasible after scientific medicine has already provided basic certainties. We must never forget that our herb-taking great-grandparents lived, on average, only half as long as we do today.

Over the course of researching and writing this book, I have come to develop a great respect for the old tradition and the people who passed it on. Indeed, how else can one speak of a body of ideas which has survived from before the days of Aristotle, was familiar to Chaucer and Elizabeth I, was defended by John Wesley, known to Thomas Hardy's peasants, purged the rich at Grafenburg and Champneys, became the inheritance of mill workers in Edwardian Salford, and in our own time has successfully transformed itself into big business? In no way is it my proposition that this tradition survived intact or as a conscious culture; but it *is* my argument that an astonishing collection of precepts concerning health, disease, and mortality has come down to us, and that this is what constitutes the Medicine of the People.

Notes and references

1 The people's health

1 G. Melvyn Howe, *Man, Environment and Disease in Britain: a Medical Geography through the Ages* (Pelican, 1976), 176, 204–206.

2 1 *Samuel*, VI.

3 Seyyed Hosein Nasr, *Islamic Science, an Illustrated Study* (London 1976), 140–141.

4 Hippocrates, *Epidemics*, Bk. l, in *The Hippocratic Writings,* transl. J. Chadwick and W.N. Mann (Penguin, 1983) 87–101, and following cases. Also Hippocrates, *Airs, Waters and Places*, in *Hippocratic Writings*, 148–170. L. Fabian Hirst, *The Conquest of Plague; a Study of the Evolution of Epidemiology* (Oxford, 1953), 35–37. Dr Thomas Shapter discussed 'aerial' and 'contagious' (person to person) theories of cholera, and sided with the aerial, or miasmic, view in *The History of Cholera in Exeter in 1832* (1849), reprinted by S.R. Publishers (Wakefield, 1971), 228–230.

5 F. Cartwright and M.D. Biddiss, *Disease and History* (London, 1972), Ch. 5, 113–136.

6 Charles Dickens, *Bleak House* (1853), Chs. XXXI and XXXV. Emile Zola, *Nana* (1880), Ch. 14, Penguin edn. (1986), 457–470. Nana's infection is perhaps the more ironic, for sixty-odd years before the period of the Second Empire, in which Zola set his story, Napoleon Bonaparte had done his best to encourage vaccination, including the mass vaccination of his Grand Armée. Even so, vaccination, especially when made compulsory by law, aroused virulent opposition in America, and to some degree in Britain, as seen in such publications as George R. Clements, *The Villainy of Vaccination and Innoculation* (Health for All Press; no date, but Bodleian Library copyright acquisition date 27 October 1927).

7   Charles Tattersall, *Annual Report of the Medical Officer of Health* (Salford, 1901), 42. For an analysis of the changing incidences of tuberculosis, bronchitis and cancer in Salford, 1900–1973, see D.J. Roberts, *Annual Report of the M.O.H.* (Salford, 1973), Graph p.9.

8   R.A. Lewis, *Edwin Chadwick and the Public Health Movement, 1832–1854*, Longmans (London, 1952).

9   John Snow, *On the Mode of Communication of Cholera* (1849), 2nd ed. 1854. The 1854 edition was reprinted in *Snow on Cholera*, with a biographical memoir by B.W. Richardson (New York, 1936).

10 William H. Duncan, *Report to the Health Committee of the Borough of Liverpool on the Health of the Town during the Years 1847,1848, 1849 and 1850* (Liverpool, 1851), tables XVII, p.83, and XIX, p.86. See also Duncan's *Report* (1857), 3.

11 Tattersall, *Annual Report* ([n.7] above). Out of a total population of 221,536, there were 6,447 people over 65: p.11. Some 624 over-65-year-olds were included in the total 4,802 recorded deaths in 1900–01: see pp.13, 15.

12 In his 1901 *Annual Reports* Dr Tattersall pointed out that Salford's death rate when compared alongside that of 32 other major cities was beaten only by Manchester with 22 deaths per 1,000 persons, and Liverpool with 22.8. For Oxford's figures see Dr Alfred Winkfield, *City of Oxford M.O.H. Report for 1901* (Oxford, 1902), 4.

13 Lawrence Stone, *The Family, Sex and Marriage in England, 1500–1800* (London, 1977), 485.

14 *The Shorter Pepys*, ed. Robert Latham (Bell and Hayman, London, 1986): 23 January 1669, p.981.

15 *Kilvert's Diary*, ed. W. Plomer, vol.1, Jonathan Cape (London, 1976): 24 December 1870, pp.285–286. Peter Ackroyd, *Dickens* (1990: Minerva, London, 1996), 601.

16 D.H. Lawrence, *Sons and Lovers* (1913), Chapter 5. Like Lawrence's fictional Nottinghamshire collier, Morel, my grandmother also said that it was common for the Pendlebury colliers of 1910 to keep their trousers on when scrubbing their bare upper bodies. Bill Naughton, *On the Pig's Back, an Autobiographical Excursion*

(Oxford University Press, 1987) 84, describes the multiple washes needed on a Saturday, and the use of Vaseline to cleanse the eyes.

17 Bill Naughton, *ibid.*, 141, says that in Bolton around World War I it was general to wear the same shirt, night and day, without removal from the body, for a week at a time.

18 It must not be forgotten, however, that Allinson's do have a genuine historical claim to being old-fashioned producers of quality bread. In 1910, for instance, they were advertising 'Allinson Wholemeal Bread' in vegetarian publications, where the nutritious properties of wholemeal as opposed to white bread were emphasised. One could also write off for a booklet on the virtues of natural flour products entitled *A Chat with Dr Allinson*, and purchasers were alerted to 'the paper band round the loaf' complete with Allinson's autograph and photograph, to certify the product's authenticity: see Dr Robert Bell, *Dietetics and Hygienics versus Disease*, Psycho-Therapeutic Society (London, 1910), a sixpenny pamphlet. The Allinson advertisement is printed on the last cover page. [Bodleian Library, 16833e14(25).]

19 All of these advertisements were seen by the author in 1987.

20 This advice, along with £50, was said to have comprised the legacy of the unnamed Greenock sage: *Consult me... by the author of 'Enquire Within'*, W. Nicholson and Sons (Pubs.) (London, 1884(?)), 72. This anonymous and undated family *vade mecum* contains a Preface dated December 1883.

21 Paul Rowlinson, 'Nineteenth-century public analysts and the adulteration of food, 1851–1880', Oxford University Chemistry Part II thesis (1977): see milk, 75; bread, 79; tea, 81; beer, 83.

22 Charles Tattersall, *Special Report On An Epidemic Of Arsenical Poisoning From Beer In 1900* (Salford, 1900). Also Rowlinson [n.21]: butter, 87; confectionery, 91.

23 Many people have told me of this practice, prevalent before World War I, and most often transacted with market traders.

24 Robert Roberts, *The Classic Slum,* Penguin (1974), 108.
25 The activities of Mrs Edwina Currie, the Junior Health Minister in the Conservative Government, 1987, aroused a massive reaction because of her dietary homilies which condemned these popular foods.
26 My aunt, Martha (*b.* 1893), said that this was a common mark of favour, bestowed by father on an obedient child in Pendlebury, Lancashire, around 1900. The same practice was also followed by the middle classes: see W. Somerset Maugham, *Of Human Bondage* (1915), Ch. 4, end.
27 G. Melvyn Howe, *op. cit.* [n.1], 205–206.
28 Elizabeth Roberts, *A Woman's Place,* Blackwell (Oxford, 1984), 30–33.
29 I still have vivid memories of the far from appetising and sloppy food served up by my grandmother and her friends in the 1950s and 1960s. Food was intended to impart bulk, and not joy.
30 This figure is cited in H.A. Allbutt's *Infant Mortality* (London, 1894), 5.
31 Rowlinson, *op. cit.* [n.21], 83.
32 I am indebted to Michael J. Clarke for drawing my attention to the opium problem in the nineteenth century, when working under my supervision for his Oxford University B.A. thesis 'A history of alkaloid drug abuse, with special reference to Britain in the period 1800–1980', unpublished Chemistry Part II thesis (1984): 8. See also M.J. Clarke, 'Suicides by opium and its derivatives, in England and Wales, 1850–1950', *Journal of Psychological Medicine* 15 (1985), 237–242. And it was not only the poor who used laudanum for their ailments. E.F. Benson's novel *Queen Lucia,* Hutchinson (1920); Black Swan Edition (London, 1986), 148, mentions its use in his fictitious upper-middle-class community of rich, leisured folk: 'She wanted a drop of laudanum and had to say what it was for [toothache], and even then she had to sign a paper', when visiting the chemist's shop.
33 G. La French 'Poisoning by Paregoric', *Pharmaceutical Journal* 4 (1845), 462. Also, Clarke, 'A history' [n.32], 8.

34 Clarke, 'A history' [n.32], 11–12. For the early history of aspirin as an analgesic after 1900, see Sophie Jourdier, 'A Miracle Drug', *Chemistry in Britain* (February, 1999), 33-35. See also Sophie Jourdier's fuller account in her 'Discovery and Development of Mild Analgesics Marketed in Britain between 1870 and 1970', Oxford University Part II Chemistry B.A. thesis (1997)

35 'Poisoning by nurse's drops – prosecution under the Pharmacy Act', *Pharmaceutical Journal* **7** (1877), 1072. Clarke, 18–19, lists several proprietary baby-soothers which relied on opiates, and their involvement in accidental deaths. Yet even an 'infants' cordial' would have been less harmful than the accidental dose of vitriol administered to five-month-old James Powel in 1836: *The Diary of Abraham Driver, Deputy Constable of Broughton (Salford), 1834–36*, ed. A. Frankland, (Salford 1973), 13 January 1836, p.13. See also John Brimble, *Pills and Potions. Folk Medicine in the Black Country* (Halesowen?, undated, *c.* 1985), 10.

36 Roberts, *Classic Slum* [n.24], 126,

37 Clarke, 'A history' [n.32], 12, 14.

38 'Observations on the improper use of opium in England', *The Lancet* **1** (1840), 382. The use of opiates by literary persons, such as De Quincey, Coleridge and others, whose activities excited no condemnation, says much for the social tolerance shown towards the Victorian drug user. See Alethea Hayter, *Opium and the Romantic Imagination,* Faber & Faber (London, 1968). The addictions in most cases derived from medical over-prescription, as with George Crabbe (for apoplexy), 165; Coleridge (neuralgia), 191; De Quincey (neuralgia and malaria), 226; and Wilkie Collins (painful eye), 255. The hallucinations only came later. See also V. Berridge and G. Edwards, *Opium and the People*, Allen Lane (London, 1981).

39 Elizabeth Gaskell, *Mary Barton, a Tale of Manchester Life* (1848); Penguin ed. (1984) 168. Also A. Calkin, *Opium and the Opium Habit* (Philadelphia, 1871), p.290, and Clarke, 'A history' [n.32],17.

40 Arthur Conan Doyle, *The Man with the Twisted Lip*, originally published as Sherlock Holmes' Adventure VI in the *Strand Magazine* in a series between July 1891 and December 1892; see *The Complete Illustrated Short Stories*, Chancellor Press (London, 1965),102.

41 Robert Tressell [Robert Noonan], *The Ragged Trousered Philanthropists* (1911), Lawrence and Wishart 1955 ed., reprinted 1985, Ch.6 p.93.

2   An immemorial tradition

1   Gaius Plinius Secundus [Pliny], *The History of the World, Commonly called the Natural History*, transl. Philemon Holland; this edition, Centaur Press (London, 1962). See under herbs, flowers, gemstones, etc.; Book XX, p.181, for the doctrine of sympathy. Like the medieval *Physiologus*, or book of beasts, which derived from Pliny, my grandfather saw nature as a teleological hierarchy filled with moral exemplars. He said that dying elephants instinctively journeyed to their 'graveyard', that lions were royal beasts, and that bees lived under a king and queen bee. The king bee is discussed by T.H. White in *A Book of Beasts*, Jonathan Cape (London, 1969), 153.

2   A.C. Crombie, *From Augustine to Galileo*, vol. 1, Penguin (1969), 90–92.

3   C. Singer and E.A. Underwood, *A Short History of Medicine*, Oxford University Press (Oxford, 1962), 16–48.

4   See the *Hippocratic Writings*, transl. J Chadwick and W.N. Mann, edited by G.E.R. Lloyd, Penguin (1983).

5   This attempt to classify nature and explain its vital processes lay at the heart of classical science. It was sometimes conceived in terms of 'atomic' or primary particles, as in Lucretius, *De Rerum Natura (On the Nature of Things)*, of *c*.58 B.C.: see Everyman ed. (1949), or Penguin (1951), Bk.1.

6 Aristotle, *De caelo* (*On the Heavens*) Bk.I Ch.2 and Bk. III Ch.5, transl. J.L. Stocks in *The Works of Aristotle*, vol.2, ed. W.D. Ross (1930), O.U.P (1966), 269b, 304a. See also Singer & Underwood, *Short History of Medicine* [n.3], 46–48, and Crombie, *Augustine to Galileo*, [n.2], 90–92.

7 Crombie, *Augustine to Galileo* [n.2], 170. Aristotle describes the formation of the four elements and their response to heat, cold, and so on, to form bone and flesh in *De partibus animalium* (*On the Parts of Animals*), 1; see W. Ogle's transl. in Ross & Clark's *The Works of Aristotle*, vol.5, 1912 (1965), 646a 1–30.

8 Galen's *De humoribus* (*On the Humours*), 1, and the relation of humours and temperaments is discussed in Percy Ansell Robin, *The Old Physiology in English Literature*, Dent & Sons (London, 1911), 37.

9 Ben Jonson, *Every Man in his Humour* (1598). The plot of this play hinges on the different 'humours', or temperaments, of the characters.

10 The doctrine of the three spirits was developed in the physiological writings of Galen (2nd century A.D.): see Singer and Underwood, *Short History of Medicine* [n.3], 63–65.

11 A good account of this theory is given by Jonathan Miller in *The Body in Question*, Macmillan (London, 1982), 185–186.

12 Aristotle, *De Partibus Animalium*, Bk. III [n.7], 670a 20.

13 These ideas about blood not only existed in classical medical textbooks, but also ran through classical poetry and satire; Virgil in *Aeneid,*V, lines 395–396, says: 'But my blood is icy and sluggish, slowed down by old age, and the strength in my body is exhausted and cold'. I am indebted to my wife Rachel for pointing out this and many other references to me, and for supplying her own translation from the original Latin.

14 William Shakespeare, *As You Like It* (*c.*1599), Act II, Sc.7.

15 The nineteenth-century physician as a classically educated gentleman is discussed in Ivan Waddington, *The Medical Profession in the Industrial Revolution*, Gill & Macmillan (Dublin, 1984), 3–4.

16 For Andreas Vesalius, *De Humani Corporis Fabrica* (*On the fabric of the human body*) (1543) see also C.D. O'Malley, *Andreas Vesalius of Brussels* (Los Angeles,1964), and J.B. de C.M. Saunders and C.D. O'Malley, *The Anatomical Drawings of Andreas Vesalius* (New York, 1982).

17 William Harvey, *De Motu Cordis et Sanguinis in Animalibus* (*On the Motion of the Heart and Blood in Animals*) (1628), transl. F.J. Franklin (Oxford, 1957). Also Kenneth D. Keele, *William Harvey, the Man, the Physician and the Scientist*, Nelson (London, 1965).

18 Vernon Coleman, *The Story of Medicine*, Robert Hale (London, 1985), 63.

19 *Thomas Willis's Oxford Lectures*, ed. Kenneth Dewhurst, Sandford (Oxford, 1980). See also K. Dewhirst, *Thomas Willis as a Physician*, University of California (1964). Margaret Espinasse, *Robert Hooke,* Heinemann (London, 1956).

20 Acceptance of the germ theory was by no means universal even towards the end of the nineteenth century, as was evident from Charles Creighton's *History of Epidemics in Britain* (1891–94).

21 See Singer and Underwood, *Short History of Medicine* [n.3], 311–12, 374, 686, 689–90.

22 Howe, *Man, Environment and Disease in Britain* [ch.1, n.1], table 9, p.212.

23 Geoffrey Chaucer, *The Nun's Priest's Tale*, in *Canterbury Tales*, transl. Sir Nevil Coghill, Penguin (1969), 235–236, where bad dreams are ascribed to choler and melancholy, and treated by purging.

24 Chaucer, *The Canon's Yeoman's Tale,* Part 1, in *Canterbury Tales* [n.23], 472–479.

25 Shakespeare, *The Merchant of Venice* (1596–1600), Act III, Sc.2.

26 *Much Ado about Nothing* (1599), Act III, Sc.2, 27. *Othello* (1604), Act III, Sc. 4, 33.

27 *Love's Labours Lost* (1598), Act V, Sc.1, 2. *King John* (1598), Act V, Sc.l, 12.

28 *Romeo and Juliet* (1597), Act IV, Sc.2. In *King Henry the Fourth*, Part II (1598), Act IV, Sc.3, Falstaff extols the virtues of sherry, which warmed the liver and blood and sent invigorating spirits to the brain.

29 Andrew Boorde, *Here Foloweth a Compendyous Regymen, or a Dyetary of Helth, made in Mountpyllier* (1545(?)) Ch. 3, fol.ci. This is a rare work, the Bodleian Library copy being in [Crynes, 837.].

30 Paul Slack is of the opinion that, while professing to aid 'poor men', many vernacular Tudor medical works would still have been too expensive and demanding to have reached them; see his 'Mirror of health and treasures of poor men: the uses of the vernacular medical literature in Tudor England' in Charles Webster (ed.), *Health, Medicine and Mortality in the Sixteenth Century*, Cambridge University Press (Cambridge, 1979), 237–275.

31 Thomas Elyot, *The Castel of Helth (1541), Preface*. Bodleian Library : [Tanner, 272 (1)]. The British Library Catalogue records the first printed edition of Elyot's *Castel* as 1539.

32 John Gerard, *The Herball, or a General Historie of Plants* (London, 1597), published in a more extensive edition, 1633, and reprinted in facsimile by Dover (New York, 1975). Agnes Arber, *Herbals, their Origin and Evolution, 1470–1670* (1912), C.U.P. (1988).

33 See Nicholas Culpeper, *The English Physician, or an Astrologo-Physical Discourse of the Vulgar Herbs of This Nation* (London, 1652). This work underwent various modifications on its basic format, and the *Culpeper's Compleat Herbal and English Physician* (London, 1826) was reprinted in facsimile in 1979 and is still in print. Before this facsimile, Foulshams had issued editions of the work in 1923, 1932, 1947, 1953 and 1961.

34 *Culpeper's Book of Birth: a Seventeenth-Century Guide to having Lusty Children*, ed. Ian Thomas, Webb & Bower (Exeter, 1986).

35 *The Regimen Sanitatis Salerni* (*The Rules of Health of Salerno*), ascribed to Arnold of Villa Nova, was one of the most influential medical compilations of the middle ages, and probably dates from the thirteenth century.

36 *Regimen Sanitas* [sic] *Salerni, this boke teachinge all people to governe them in helthe, as translated out of the Latyne tonge in to Englyshe by Thomas Paynel* (London, 1541), Bodleian Library copy [Tanner, 272] .

37 Sir Thomas More, in the early sixteenth century, estimated that nearly half the population of London was literate to some extent, a fact borne out by several commentators; see Antonia McLean, *Humanism and the Rise of Science in Tudor England*, Heinemann (London, 1972), 82.

38 Bernard Capp, *Astrology and the Popular Press, English Almanacs 1500–1800*, Faber (London,1979), 204–214. A. Chapman, 'Astrological Medicine', in Webster (ed.), *Health, Medicine and Mortality* [n.30], 275–300.

39 *A Midsummer Night's Dream* (1595–96), Act III, Sc. 2.

40 Anthony Askham, for instance, described himself as 'Phisition' in his 1551 almanac, and 'Priest' in 1557; see Bodleian Library copies [80 C. 226 Art.]

41 Charles Webster, *The Great Instauration. Science, Medicine and Reform 1626–1660*, Duckworth (London, 1975), Ch.IV.

42 G.A. Lindeboom, *Herman Boerhaave, the Man and his Work,* Methuen (London, 1968), 274–275.

43 Thomas Hobbes, *Leviathan* (1651), Introduction, ed. C.B. Macpherson, Penguin (1968), 81.

44 John Wesley, *Primitive Physick, or the Easy and Natural Way of Curing Most Diseases* (London, 1747). I have cited from the 'Preface' of the 5th edition (Bristol, 1755), Para.8–9, p.viii. The London 1775 edition was reprinted under the title *Primitive Remedies*, Howard B. Weeks (ed.), Woodbridge Press, Santa Barbara, California (1971), 'Preface', Para. 8. This is to my knowledge the only edition currently in print .

45 The *National Union Catalog* (1969) of the American Library Association also lists known editions of *Primitive Physick* from 1845, 1847, 1852, 1854, 186–?, 1860?, 1869?, 1870?, and an American edition of 1858.

46 Though *De Generatione Animalium* (On the Generation of Animals) forms the core of *Aristotle's Works*, fragments of other authentic Aristotelian writings are also

incorporated, such as his *De Partibus Animalium* [n.7], and *Historia Animalium* (*An Account of Animals*). Between them, they comprised the best system of biology and physiology to come out of ancient Greece. In addition to the fragments of the genuine writings of Aristotle incorporated into the pseudo-Aristotelian *Works*, however, there was a general miscellany of later classical and medieval ideas on reproduction, medicine and physiology. Fragments borrowed from Galen – especially his humoral doctrines – were also incorporated, along with a number of 'old wives' tales' in common circulation. In short, *Aristotle's Works* was a polyglot compilation in which the name and writings of Aristotle (always deferred to as 'The Philosopher') were used as a stem upon which to graft a diversity of antique medical ideas. The early history of *Aristotle's Works* is dealt with by Janet Blackman in 'Popular Theories of Generation: the Evolution of *Aristotle's Works*. The Story of an Anachronism', in *Health Care and Popular Medicine in Nineteenth-Century England*, ed. John Woodward and David Richards, Croom Helm (London, 1977),56–88.

47 The American *National Union Catalog* [n.45] also lists many recorded copies of *Aristotle's Works*, dating from 1733. Both the *British Library Catalogue* and American *National Union Catalog* record related, or component, parts of the *Works* such as *Aristotle's Compleat Midwife* (Nat. Un. Cat. earliest dated copy 1700), and *Aristotle's Masterpiece*, with references to 1684. The pseudo-Aristotelian *Works* in their various forms have been ascribed on some of the title pages of preserved copies to one William Salman or Salmon (1644–1713?), though the original format is much older.

48 Henry A. Allbutt, *Disease and Marriage* (London 1891), p.iv; see also 'Preface'.

49 Alice Bunker Stockham, M.D., *Tokology: A Book for Every Woman* (London, 1918): see *British Library Catalogue* and *Union Catalog* for earlier printing history.

50 *Revised Edition of the Works* of Aristotle the Famous *Philosopher, containing his complete Masterpiece and*

Family Physician, his Experienced Midwife, his Book of Problems and Remarks on Physiognomy..... published by J. Smith, High Holborn (London, 1857), 262. I am indebted to Mrs J. Bagshaw of Carnforth for the loan of this copy. The authentic Aristotle considered the heart to be the true seat of life and blood, though the liver also played a vital generative part: see *De Partibus Animalium* [n.7], Bk.II, 2, 670a, 20–25. The primacy of the heart and liver derived from their early appearance in the chick embryo, Bk. III, 4, 665a, 30. Aristotle himself was uncertain about the relation between veins and arteries, and how they entered and left the heart. He considered that the right ventricle held the hottest blood, and the left the coldest, thereby accounting for the belief that the right-hand side of the body was warmer than the left; *De Partibus Animalium*, [n.7], Bk III, 4, 667a, 1 ff. Most of Book III is devoted to the relation between blood and respiration. See also the extensive explanatory footnotes in Ogle's translation, *op. cit.* The assumption that women are colder than men (or females colder than males) underlies the whole of Aristotle's biology, as in *De Generatione Animalium*, Bk.II. The belief that breast milk was a diverted, or 'concocted', menstrual discharge in pregnant *mammals* is explained in *De Generatione Animalium*, Bk.II, 4, 739b, 20–25. Within the overall context of Aristotle's biology, it was possible to derive or deduce things which the philosopher did not necessarily mention as such, yet were congruent with the principles of the system. Such modes of reasoning formed part of that quasi-classical fabric of old wives' tales which accounted for so many of the physiological explanations in *Aristotle's Works* between the late seventeenth and early twentieth centuries. In a very late copy of the *Works* in the Radcliffe Science Library, Oxford, R.S.L 15073 g.2, *The Works of Aristotle the Famous philosopher*, undated (London, *c.*1900), the hoary old favourites are still present: women's blood is thicker than men's because the coldness of women makes it congeal more easily, 383; men's 'seed' is white because their greater heat refines it from blood, 387; and blood comes from the liver and enters the veins and not the arteries, 382.

51 *Aristotle's Works* (1857) [n.50], 270.
52 *Aristotle's Works* (1857) [n.50], 119. This remedy comes from the section entitled 'The Family Physician, being choice and approved remedies'. It was a popular 'cure', and appeared in several editions of the *Works* which I examined, such as *The Works of Aristotle the Famous Philosopher* [n.50],167
53 A.L. Rowse, *A Cornishman at Oxford*, Jonathan Cape (London, 1965),196.
54 Will E. Haines and Jimmy Harper, 'In my little bottom drawer', (1934), Cameo Publishing Co., Campbell Connolly & Co., Ltd, London. The song was performed in the film *Sing As We Go* (1934). The words have undergone variations, however, and in Gracie Fields' rendition in the recording *Amazing Gracie* (1985), Savile CSUL 170, Conifer Records Ltd, the reference to *Aristotle's Works* has been replaced by 'Priestley's Works'. This may have resulted either from the risqué nature of Aristotle, or from the increasing obsolescence, and hence meaninglessness, to subsequent generations by the time of Gracie Fields' later recordings. The recording date of the songs on *Amazing Gracie* is not given, though she sounded an old lady. I had some difficulty tracing an early version of the score which mentions Aristotle, and I am indebted to two people who both independently located it for me. I thank Mr Derek Stott of Worsley, and the late Miss Marti Caine, whom I heard perform the song on television and who kindly supplied me with a correct score. The authentic words to 'In my little bottom drawer', and the reference to *Aristotle's Works*, are to be found in *Our Gracie* (1978), E.M.I. Music Publishing Co., 138–140 Charing Cross Rd., London pp.12–13.
55 *Consult Me* [ch.1, n.20], 'To the reader'.
56 Hippocrates placed great stress on location and climate as factors central to health and disease: see *Airs, Waters and Places*, in *The Hippocratic Writings* [ch.1, n.4], 148–169.
57 Isabella Beeton, *The Book of Household Management* (London, 1869); see 'The Doctor', 1093–1124, para. 2709.

3 The pathology of the people:
a popular explanation for disease

1 Blood was generated from food, and formed bile and phlegm by the agency of heat: Galen, *On the Natural Faculties* Bk. II, 9, transl. Arthur J. Brock, published in *Great Books of the Western World*, R.M. Hutchins (ed.), *Encyclopaedia Britannica* (Chicago, 1952), 197–198. For an account of Galen's ideas on blood, see Crombie, *Augustine to Galileo*, 1 [ch.2, n.2], 172.

2 See Hippocrates, *The Nature of Man*, transl. J. Chadwick and W.N. Mann, in *The Hippocratic Writings* [ch.1, n.4], 260–271.

3 Aristotle discusses the active–passive roles of men and women in *De Generatione Animalium* [ch.2, n.50], Bk. I, 21, 729b 5–10; Bk. II, 14, 739a 30 and 739b 1–15; Bk IV, 3, 766b 10–30.

4 Bloodletting was used extensively in Tudor medicine, and is discussed in such popular works of the period as Thomas Buckminster, *A New Almanack and Prognostication* (London, 1589), which contains the 'rules' of bloodletting along with a picture of the 'zodiac man', showing which signs govern which parts of the body. Bodleian Library copy [Ashmole, 1589 f.1].

5 Ronald W. Clark, *The Survival of Charles Darwin*, Random House (New York, 1984), 173–174.

6 For an account of these experiments, see Marjorie H. Nicholson, *Pepys's Diary and the New Philosophy*, University of Virginia (Charlottesville, 1965), 53–92. See also Coleman, *Story of Medicine* [ch.2, n.18], 190. Singer and Underwood, *Short history of Medicine,* [ch.2, n.3], 698–701.

7 Francis Galton discusses predispositions to criminality, alcoholism and madness in *Inquiries into Human Faculty and its Development* (1883), Everyman edition, undated (*c.*1910); see 'Criminals and the Insane', 42–47. Also G.F. Drinka, *The Birth of Neurosis: Myth, Malady and the Victorians*, Simon Schuster (New York, 1984), 49–53.

8   The use of the phrase 'cut the phlegm' is one of the most widely encountered terms received from my respondents.

9   Related to me by Miss M. of Salford, 1986, who had received it from her own mother who had lived from 1890 to 1982.

10 My grandmother (born 1892) swore that a well-rubbed and swathed chest provided protection against most diseases.

11 Related by my mother (born 1913).

12 My mother related this story to me, for though she was only eight years old at the time, she said that it formed a vivid memory. The boy in question was the son of a neighbour in New Street, Pendlebury, Lancashire, and my mother subsequently received a full account of the incident from her mother.

13 William Fox, *The Working Man's Model Family Botanic Guide, or Every Man his own Doctor*, 10th edition (Sheffield, 1884). See four elements and getting rid of poisons, 10; Steam Engine Physiology, 10–15, 16,17. As in his 'Preface' to *The Working Man's Model* Fox claimed that 30,000 copies of the book had been sold in the previous nine editions, one can estimate the extent to which one single quack publication could help to re-affirm and pass on the Medicine of the People. See also F.B. Smith, *The People's Health* (Croom Helm, London, 1979), 340, for the Coffinite Dispensary in Oldham.

14 Richard Mead, *A Treatise Concerning the Influence of the Sun and Moon upon Human Bodies, and the Diseases Thereby Produced*, (London, 1748).

15 Lyell Watson, *Supernature, a Natural History of the Supernatural*, Hodder & Stoughton (London, 1973), Part 1.

16 *The Works of Aristotle the Famous Philosopher*, undated (London *c*.1900), 368. This copy in is Oxford [R.S.L. 15073 g.2]. The genuine Aristotle ascribed menstruation to the cooling influence of the waning Moon, *De Generatione Animalium* [ch.2, n.7], Bk. II, 4, 738a 15. In *Historia Animalium* (Account of Animals), Aristotle said menstruation usually occurred towards the end of the lunar month, though it was mainly 'wiseacres' who

affirmed the lunar cause: Bk.II, 2. See D'Arcy Wentworth Thompson's transl., in *The Works of Aristotle*, vol.4, ed. Smith and Ross, 1910 (O.U.P, 1967), 582a 30; 582b 1. Though discounting the lunar cause of menstruation in 1912, Arthur Platt, the translator of *De Generatione Animalium,* nonetheless adds the more recent comments in its favour, such as those of Mead, Darwin and Huxley: see Smith and Ross (eds.), *The Works of Aristotle*, vol.V, 1912 (O.U.P. 1965), 738a 15, footnote 3.

17 John Camp, *Magic, Myth and Medicine*, Priory Press (London, 1971) 41.

18 *Aristotle's Works* (1857) [ch.2,n.50], 287–312. Shakespeare, *The Tempest* (1611), Act II, Sc.2. The fascination with physiognomy and 'monsterous births' always formed key sections in Victorian editions of *Aristotle's Works*. They did possess a clear lineage back to the authentic Aristotle, however: *De Generatione Animalium* [n.16], Bk. IV, 3, 769b ff., discusses deformities (monsters), while *Historia Animalium* [n.16], Bk. VII, 6, 585b 30–35 and 586a 1, looks at the problems of heredity.

19 R.S. Stevenson, 'The insanity of George III', *Famous Illnesses in History*, Eyre & Spottiswoode (London, 1962), 154–171. The eighteenth-century quack, James Graham, had used electrical cures, as had Elisha Perkins in New York: see Eric Maple, *Magic, Medicine and Quackery*, Robert Hale (London, 1968), 118, 138. The Museum of the History of Science, Oxford, contains a large collection of eighteenth- and nineteenth-century electro-medical devices. For the most authoritative study of George III's episodes of mental illness, and their influence upon medical and social attitudes to the same diseases in others, see Ida Macalpine and Richard Hunter, *George III and the Mad-Business* (Pimlico, London, 1993, 1995).

20 Hippocrates attributed many fevers to changed states of the air, as occasioned by the seasons; see *Aphorisms*, Section III, in *The Hippocratic Writings* [ch.1, n.4], 213–216. Thomas Shapter mentioned a cholera victim in

1832, attributing his disease to having 'smelt effluvia at a funeral', in *The History of the Cholera in Exeter in 1832* [ch.1, n.4], 229.

21 D.H. Lawrence, *Sons and Lovers* (1913), Ch. 4, Penguin (1959), 472.

22 Tressell, *The Ragged Trousered Philanthropists* (1914) [ch.1, n.41], ch.52, p.614.

23 Thomas Hardy, *Tess of the D'Urbervilles* (1891), Phase 1, III; Penguin (1978), 59. See also Ruth A. Frior, *Folkways in Thomas Hardy* (1931), Perpetua edition, Barnes; New York (1962), 109–124.

24 Mr B. of Manchester. His mother was born in 1882. Private communication, 4 January 1987.

25 *Aristotle's Works* (1857) [ch.2, n.50], 132–134. Similar pre-Aristotelian ideas are discussed in, *Embryology and Anatomy*, transl. I.M. Lonie, in *The Hippocratic Writings* [ch.1, n.4], 317–346, where the crucial temperature differences between the sexes are discussed.

26 *Aristotle's Works* (1857) [ch.2, n.50], 64–65.

27 *Aristotle's Works*, 208.

28 *Aristotle's Works*, 259.

29 *Aristotle's Works*, 263, 266.

30 *Aristotle's Works*, 267, 268.

31 *Aristotle's Works*, 269. The cause and classification of dreams produced an enormous literature in the ancient and medieval worlds. Hippocrates, in *Regimen* IV, 'Dreams', discusses them: see *The Hippocratic Writings* [ch.1, n.4], 252–259, as do Macrobius and others. On a literary level, Chaucer discusses them in *The House of Fame*, Bk.1, Proem, and in *The Nun's Priest's Tale*, Coghill transl., Penguin (1969), 235–236. The ascription of bad dreams to food also possessed a long lineage. In Charles Dickens' *A Christmas Carol* (1843), Stave 1, Scrooge tries to dismiss Marley's ghost as an hallucination produced by an undigested meal.

32 A senior member of the Bodleian Library, Oxford, told me that as a schoolboy in Bristol, during the 1940s, he remembered the book on sale in a 'prohibited' shop, where its contents provided material for juvenile speculation.

33 W. George, *Words of Wisdom on Courtship and Marriage*, undated (*c*.1890). Price 6 [old] pence Bodleian Library pamphlet [24762 e 5].

34 John M. Robertson, *Over-population, A Lecture*, (London, 1890). Bodleian Library pamphlet [24762 e 5].

35 H.A. Allbutt, *The Wife's Handbook* (London, 1886), Price sixpence. See 'Introduction'. By *c*.1900, however, even updated versions of *Aristotle Works*, which had been castigated by Allbutt in *Diseases of Marriage* (London, 1891), p.iv, were coming to include sections on 'Ways and means of prevention', as well as carrying advertisements for birth control devices. See *The Works of Aristotle the famous Philosopher*, by 'The Booksellers' (London, *c*.1900). This particular copy of Aristotle is not the same as the other *c*.1900 copy cited elsewhere in this book. Both this and the other *c*. 1900 copy are very similar in typeface, illustrations, binding and other details, but there are significant differences, such as the inclusion of birth control information in one, and not in the other. It is also in the Radcliffe Science Library, Oxford [R.S.L. 15073 g 3]. This latter *Aristotle's Works* commences with a section on 'The population question', and prints a letter from Lady Florence Dixie, 5 November 1890, advocating birth control. See also 517–521.

36 Popular birth control publications began to appear in the wake of Francis Place's *To the Married of Both Sexes* (1823); see Norman Himes, *Medical History of Contraception*, Allen & Unwin (London, 1936), 212–223. For contraception in Edwardian Salford, see Roberts, *The Classic Slum*, [ch.1, n.24], 51–52, 205, 231, 232.

4 Popular remedies and procedures

1   The popularity of purges was not only deeply entrenched in folk medicine, but up to the nineteenth century had been an essential prerequisite to most cures in academic medicine also. The casebooks of the seventeenth-century Stratford physician Dr John Hall indicate extensive use:

see his *Select Observations on English Bodies* (London, 1679), published in *Shakespeare's son-in-law: John Hall, Man and Physician*, ed. Harriet Joseph (1976). No publisher cited.

2   Charles Dickens, *Life and Adventures of Nicholas Nickleby* (1838–39), Chapter VIII; Oxford Illustrated Dickens ed. (O.U.P.–1950), 88–89.

3   Information given in the television Programme 'John Evans at 108', BBC2 television, 17 August 1986.

4   Sulphur is also cited by Eunice Schofield in *Medical Care of the Working Class in 1900*, Federation of Local History Societies in Lancashire (1979), 9.

5   Dr G., who qualified in Scotland and went into general practice in Bolton in the late 1930s. Private communication. (Not the same person as 'Dr W.S. Garden' cited in [ch.5 n.20].

6   Mr Jack Watkins, born in South Wales around 1900, but employed on the Lancashire coalfield most of his working life. Private communication, undated, *c*.1980.

7   D.H. Lawrence, *Sons and Lovers* (1913) [ch.3, n.21],60.

8   *Secret Remedies, What They Cost and What They Contain*, British Medical Association (London, 1909). The exotic African or American Indian source of 'secret' medicines is stressed in the 'Preface', pp. v–viii. The book analyses a wide range of popular cure-alls, revealing their chemical content and the cost of manufacture compared with their selling price. Most preparations cost under threepence to make, yet sell for more than one shilling. *Secret Remedies* is also significant in so far as it prints the label details of most of the medicines analysed, and one cannot help but note the classical physiological principles in accordance with which they were thought to work. Great stress was placed on the liver, blood, and blood purification. One is left to assume that 'secret remedy' manufacturers were familiar with customer theories of disease, and of how a cure was expected to work.

9   Michael J. Clarke, 'A history of alkaloid drug abuse' [ch.1, n.32], 55–58.

10 Roberts, *The Classic Slum* [ch.1, n.24], 125.

11 One popular formula for a cough medicine was two-pennyworth of liquorice, two-pennyworth of buckthorn, three-pennyworth of chlorodyne. The mix could be made up on request by a druggist on Regent Road, Salford, in the 1930s, and taken away in the customer's own cup or bottle. Private communication from Mrs E. of Salford, September, 1986.

12 This was related by my grandfather about the cough preparation made and sold by the Pendlebury, Manchester, chemist Teddy Banks.

13 Elizabeth Roberts, 'Oral history investigation of disease and its management by the Lancashire working class, 1890–1939', in *Health, Disease and Medicine in Lancashire 1750–1950*, ed. J.V. Pickstone, Department of Science and Technology, University of Manchester (1980), 46.

14 Sin-eating is discussed in T.M. Owen, *Welsh Folk Customs*, National Folk Museum of Wales (Cardiff, 1959), 183–184. Salt or 'flete' is mentioned in the 'fire, fleet and candle lighte' of the medieval' 'Lyke Wake Dirge': *The New Oxford Book of English Verse*, O.U.P. (1979), 368. For salt as 'fleet', see *O.E.D.* 'flet' for derivation.

15 See 'sweal' and 'swale', *O.E.D.*

16 Mr B. of Manchester, formerly of Birmingham. Private communication, 4 January 1987.

17 Lawrence, *Sons and Lovers* [ch.3, n.21], 456.

18 Related by Mr R.B., a retired surgeon of St Helen's, Lancashire. Private communication, 28 May 1987.

19 Schofield, *Medical Care of the Working Class*, [n.4], 11.

20 *Consult Me* (1883) [ch.1, n.20], 'To the reader'.

21 I am indebted to Mrs V.G. Bell, of the Salford Local History Society, for a transcription of the recipes in her great-grandmother's (1849–1919) notebook. Private communication, 1986.

22 Anne Secord, 'Science in the Pub: Artisan Botanists in Early Nineteenth-Century Lancashire', *History of Science* XXXII (1994), 269–315.

23 W. Aloysius Browne and Henry Browne, *The 'Walpole' Botanic Guide to Health* (Southampton?, *c*.1930), 3.

Copy in author's possession, for which I am indebted to
Mrs Janet McCallum, of Burscough, Lancashire.

24 Browne and Browne, *'Walpole' Botanic Guide*, 17–20.

25 *'Walpole' Botanic Guide*, 53.

26 *'Walpole' Botanic Guide*, 92.

27 *'Walpole' Botanic Guide*, 96.

28 *'Walpole' Botanic Guide*, 92. It advises 'Buy the
beautiful *Reminiscences of an Old Physician*, Dr Robert
Bell, M.D., F.R.C.P., published by John Murray (any
bookseller will get it for you)'.

29 Browne, *'Walpole' Botanic Guide*, p.92. On p.91 are
advertised the 'Walpole special cancer herbs'.

30 Schofield, *Medical Care of the Working Class* [n.4],
10–18 Roberts, *Classic Slum* [ch.1, n.24], 126–127. The
popularity of Morison's, Holloway's, Boot's and
Beecham's preparations, and the profits which they
generated, are discussed in F.B. Smith, *The People's
Health, 1830–1900*, Croom Helm (London, 1979), 343 ff.

31 Schofield [n.4], 14.

32 Alfred Fennings, *Fennings' Everybody's Doctor; or, when
ill, how to get well* (Cowes, Isle of Wight(?) *c.*1900).
Copy in author's possession, for which I am indebted to
Mrs Bunnell-Walker of Worsley, Manchester.

33 *Fennings'* [n.32], front cover.

34 *Fennings'*, 29,37.

35 *Fennings'*, 30.

36 *Fennings'*, 23.

37 *Fennings'*, inside cover. The use of the 'Government
Stamp' and the profit which it generated is discussed in
Smith, *The People's Health* [n.30], 345.

38 The *Walpole* and *Fennings'* patent medicine booklets list
the prices of their respective preparations. I am also
indebted to Mrs Georgina Kelly, née Lundie Smith, for
her recollections of the prices of many herbal
preparations sold in her father's shop around the time of
World War I. The Beecham price was encapsulated in
A.A. Francis' *A Guinea a Box (a Biography of Thomas
Beecham)* (1984). For a comprehensive study of patent
medicine prices in 1909, see the B.M.A.'s *Secret*

Remedies [n.8], where the manufacturing and selling costs are given.

39 Tressell, *The Ragged Trousered Philanthropists* [ch.1, n.41], 603.

40 John Burnett, *A History of the Cost of Living,* Penguin (1969), 253.

41 Related by Mrs Georgina Kelly [n.38], born 1898. For further details, see Chapter 5, [n.24].

42 Though it was John who baptised with water, *John* I:26, and Christ with the Holy Ghost, *John* I:33, several of Jesus' miracles nonetheless had aquatic associations, such as the driving out of Legion's many devils into pigs which subsequently drowned themselves: *Luke* VIII:32–33. Christ also anointed the eyes of the blind and the ears of the deaf with his spittle, *Mark* VII:33, and VIII: 23. Water was sometimes the agent of traditional Jewish miracles, as in the case of those who resorted to the pool at Bethesda, *John* V: 2–9.

43 See Sir James Clark, *The Sanative Influences of Climate* (London, 1841), 344–352. This work, by a leading early Victorian physician and consultant to the Royal Family, spoke of climate and water in a manner strongly reminiscent of Hippocrates' *Airs, Waters and Places.* The popularity of watering places and their respective merits was discussed in minute detail by Dr A.B. Granville, in *The Spas of England,* 2 vols. (London, 1841). See also E.S. Turner, *Taking the Cure,* Michael Joseph (London, 1967).

44 Trevor M. Cook, *Samuel Hahnemann, the Founder of Homeopathic Medicine,* Thorson Publishers Ltd. (Wellingborough, 1981).

45 The intellectual foundation of homeopathy was based on the assumption that if a drug or salt produced a symptom of sickness in a healthy person, then the same drug would counteract the same symptom when given to a sick person. Thus a drug which would induce vomiting in a healthy person would cure a person with a vomiting sickness.

46 *Catalogue of the Library of the Liverpool Medical Institution, with the Laws and a List of Members* (Liverpool, 1861). Rule II explicitly excluded homeopaths from membership of the Institution.

47 See A. Chapman, 'Medical art and experimental science in early Victorian England', being the 150th Anniversary Lecture of the Liverpool Medical Institution building, 28 May 1987: in *Transactions and Report, 1986–87*, of the L.M.I. (Liverpool, 1987), 26–39: 31–32.

5 Doctors, druggists, dentists and quacks

1 The growing professionalisation of medicine, and the intellectual and legal definition of 'doctors' as a body, are dealt with by Ivan Waddington, *The Medical Profession in the Industrial Revolution*, Gill & Macmillan (Dublin, 1984).

2 Waddington [n.1], Section II. For the significance and conditions of the Apothecaries Act in defining the professional status of the G.P., see Irvine Loudon, *Medical Care and the General Practitioner, 1750–1850*, Clarendon Press (Oxford, 1986), 167–188.

3 Roberts, *Classic Slum* [ch.1, n.24], 124.

4 John Cule, *A Doctor for the People*, Update Books (London, 1980), 115–122.

5 The scheme covered all workers between 16 and 70 years old who earned less than £160 p.a. In 1914, there were 13,689,000 persons covered, and in 1938, some 19,706,000, by which time the ceiling had been raised to £250 p.a. See Pauline Gregg, *A Social and Economic History of Britain, 1760–1965*, Harrap (London, 1965), 484.

6 Roberts, *Classic Slum* [ch.1, n.24], 124. My grandmother had vivid memories of a young Edwardian G.P. in the Pendlebury of her childhood, who rode around the cobbled streets with his black bag strapped to the carrier of his bicycle.

7 Howe, *Man, Environment and Disease* [ch.1, n.1], 205–206.

8 The German Welfare System had been greatly admired by David Lloyd George, who had visited Germany to examine it in 1908; see Thomas Jones, *Lloyd George* (O.U.P., 1951), 36–42, and John Grigg, *Lloyd George, the People's Champion, 1902–1911*, Eyre Methuen (London, 1978), 163, 337, 351.

9 See John Woodward, *To do the Sick no Harm; a Study of the British Voluntary Hospital System to 1875.* Routledge & Kegan Paul (London, 1974), 36–44.

10 Elsie Oman, *Salford Stepping Stones*, Neil Richardson (Swinton, Manchester,1983), 76.

11 The tuberculosis bacillus was identified by Robert Koch in 1882, thereby enabling its mode of transmission to be understood. This discovery made it possible to develop preventive measures to contain the disease, though an effective cure for those who had already contracted it was not feasible until the 1940s. C. and P. Barlow, *Robert Koch*, Great Nobel Prize Winners, Heron Books (Geneva, 1971), 73–75. See also Singer and Underwood, *Short History of Medicine* [ch.2, n.3], 422–424.

12 Oman, *Salford Stepping Stones* [n.10], 76.

13 Oman, p.76.

14 Gregg, *Social and Economic History of Britain* [n.5], 180–192.

15 Charles Dickens, *A Christmas Carol* (1843), Stave 1.

16 See John Grigg, 'Lloyd George', in *Founders of the Welfare State*, ed. Paul Barker, Heinemann (London, 1984), 68–74.

17 Elizabeth Roberts, 'Oral history investigations of disease' [ch.4, n.13], 40.

18 Exact medical incomes are not easy to ascertain, though from evidence supplied by various medical schools to a government committee in 1878, it was to be expected that a G.P. after ten years in practice could make around £1,000 p.a.; see Waddington, *Medical Profession in the Industrial Revolution* [n.1], 150–152. The incomes of G.P.s and consultants before 1850 is discussed in Loudon, *Medical Care and the General Practitioner* [n.2], 256–266, while Walter Rivington gives the scale by which fee-paying middle-class patients were charged in *The Medical Profession, an Essay* (Dublin, 1879), 52.

19 Dr Buck Ruxton, the Lancaster physician who won notoriety in 1935 by murdering and dismembering the bodies of his wife and maidservant, enjoyed enormous local popularity. So regarded was Dr Ruxton by his patients, many of whom were unemployed, that they addressed a petition, requesting clemency, to the Home Secretary. When I was at Lancaster University in the late 1960s I knew a college porter named Ron who as a boy had been a patient and beneficiary of Dr Ruxton, and spoke of him in the warmest terms. Dr Ruxton gave regular treats to the children of the poor, including charabanc outings and teas. Ron said that among the poor of Lancaster, Dr Ruxton's double murder (especially of his wife, who was 'no more than a tart') was regarded as nothing other than a minor flaw of character when compared alongside his charitable works.

20 This was Dr W.S. Garden of Salford. I was given this information by his grandson sometime around 1968. Dr Garden no doubt felt fully justified in charging for his services when he felt that the patient could afford them, as he was one of the most highly qualified medical men in Salford. According to the General Medical Council's *Medical Register* (1940) Dr Garden had first qualified in 1902, and held the degrees of M.B., Ch.B., and M.D. of the University of Aberdeen.

21 Elizabeth Roberts, 'Oral history investigations of disease', [Ch.4, n.13], 38–39.

22 Elizabeth Roberts discusses the survival of the untrained midwife in north Lancashire in 'Oral history', 41–44. Bill Naughton commented on their survival in the poor districts of south London during World War II, in *On the Pig's Back* [ch.1, n.16], 37.

23 The statutory history, charter and similar constitutional details of late nineteenth-century British pharmacy are to be found in *The Calendar of the Pharmaceutical Society of Great Britain* (London, 1900), 9–19 ff.

24 I am indebted to Mrs Georgina Kelly (née Lundie Smith) for this information which was related to me in a personal interview in September 1987. Mr Edward Lundie Smith,

her father, does not appear in the *Calendar of the Pharmaceutical Society*, though Charles Clegg Smith of Didsbury, whom I understand was also a member of her family, does. He received the Minor Certificate, No. 11494: p.407. As Edward Lundie Smith never qualified, and never took either the Major or Minor Certificate of the Society, he would not have appeared on the Register.

25 This was a common Lancashire phrase. Bill Naughton, in *On the Pig's Back* [ch.1, n.16], 81, said that false teeth had already become fashionable in Bolton by 1916.

26 This information was given to me many years ago, before I had begun to systematically record folk medical ideas. I can recall neither the doctor's name nor his whereabouts, though the information, as it stood, made a firm impression in my mind. I am also indebted to Dr Christine Hillam, of the University of Liverpool, for drawing my attention to much early dental material in Lancashire.

27 Home dentistry at this period, however, was probably made easier to perform as a consequence of the pyorrhoea and other gum-softening diseases occasioned by bad diet and poor oral hygiene.

28 *Calendar of the Pharmaceutical Society* (1900), [n.23], 302. Edward Banks held the Society's Minor Certificate, No. 1756. His qualifying date is given in the Society's Register for 1882.

29 'John Evans at 108', BBC2 documentary, 17 August 1986.

30 Beeton, *Book of Household Management* (1869 ed.), 2809, 2810.

31 Rivington, *The Medical Profession* [n.18], 90, 91–92.

32 Rivington, 94–95.

33 Rivington, 93.

34 Rivington, 90.

35 Related to me by Mr C. in Eccles, Lancashire, May 1984. There had also been a 'Doctor Catlin' who practised on Bilston, Staffordshire, market at some unspecified date, but probably around 1900. He also had an 'unusual mode of dress', and Indian squaws, and sold prairie herbs reminiscent of Sequah: John Brimble, *Pills and Potions: Folk Medicine in the Black County* (Halesowen(?), undated, *c*.1985), 10,

cited from J. Freeman, *Black Country Stories and Sketches* (no further publication details).

36 B.R. Townsend, 'Sequah', *The Dental Record*, vol. LX, No.10 (October 1949), 404.

37 Townsend, 405.

38 Townsend, 405.

39 The Galen claim seems to have been recorded during a visit of the 'authentic' Sequah medicine show to Egypt in the 1880s: see Townsend, 'Sequah', 406, and John Walker, *Folk Medicine in Modern Egypt,* Luzac & Co. (London, 1934), 88.

40 Related to me by an unnamed gentleman in Eccles, 9 May 1984. This gentleman was a member of the audience of a lecture which I gave to the Eccles and District Historical Society on 'The Medicine of the People', in May 1984.

41 Vivian de sola Pinto, *Enthusiast and Wit: a Portrait of John Wilmot, Earl of Rochester, 1647–1680,* Routledge & Kegan Paul (London, 1962), 82–83. The Earl of Rochester's antics as a quack also reappeared in Victorian literature, when W. Harrison Ainsworth re-created them in *Old Saint Paul's* (1841): see 'Book the Second', Chapter III, 'The quack doctors'.

42 Browne and Browne, *'Walpole' Botanic Guide* [ch.4, n.23], 114–116.

43 E.M. Ruddock, *Vitalogy, an Encyclopaedia of Health and Home* (Chicago, 1930): see plates and pages, 865–866.

44 Townsend, 'Sequah' [n.36], 408.

45 Townsend, 407.

46 John Dade's *Almanack and Prognostication for 1591* Bodleian Library [4°F, 2(6) Art /B/5] contains the following rhyme under 'For letting of blood':
   'The moone in age, the ancient sort,
   Their veynes may open best;
   The younger sort tyll moone be newe,
   Must let their veynes have rest.'

47 Eric Maple, *Magic, Medicine and Quackery,* Robert Hale (London, 1968), 99–100. Also see *D.N.B.*, 'Greatrakes'.

48 Maple [n.47] 99–100 for seventh sons; also Maple 35–59 and 83–110.

49 Mrs Sally Mapp, the eighteenth-century folk bone-setter,

is discussed in John Camp, *Myth, Magic and Medicine,* Priory Press (London 1971),135–138.

50 Account of wart-charming: Eileen Oliver to A. Chapman, Oxford, 22 March 1988.

51 For the possible correlation between faith and healing, see Camp, Ch. 8, on 'Faith and healing', 105–120. The front page of the *Oxford Courier* newspaper, 21 January 1988, carried the story of the 67-year-old Mrs Elsie Rutter miraculously healed of a crippling back complaint of ten years standing, by the Rev. P. Scothern in Oxford Town Hall.

52 See Revd Stephen Parsons, *The Challenge of Christian Healing,* SPCK (1987), and Frances Parsons, *Pools of Fresh Water. A Story of Healing,* Triangle, SPCK (1987).

53 Misdiagnosis of mental illness as possession by demons can do lasting damage. I know one lady – a Cambridge graduate and a lawyer – with a history of depressive illness, who in the early 1980s fell under the influence of a charismatic church which practised the expulsion of 'demons' in an uncontrolled and inappropriate manner. Her illness was greatly aggravated by the sense of guilt and inadequacy which such treatment entailed. Although she has been in receipt of long-term psychiatric help, the importance of which she does not underestimate, she still feels that her healing did not really begin until she managed to break away from the church in question and find a new spiritual life and mental peace in a 'sane', mainstream, non-charismatic Christian congregation.

54 St Mark's Gospel, Chapter V.

55 The title 'doctor' can still unleash curious expectations from people who hear it, who generally assume that its possessor is a medical person. When I received my Oxford D.Phil. degree in 1978, several of my mother's friends assumed that I had acquired healing powers. One lady, who was then about eighty years old, and had a work-shy, middle-aged son, asked my mother 'Does this mean he can sign sick notes for our poor Billy's [Social Security] benefit?'

6 Naturopathy, Diet Reform and the origins of alternative medicine

1   Peter Ackroyd, *Dickens* (1990; Minerva ed., London, 1996) contains numerous references to Dickens' long walks. He liked to walk each day between 2 p.m. and 5 p.m., at a regular 4¹/₂ miles per hour: p.592.

2   'The Vegetarian Society. Established in 1847', printed on the back cover of Thomas Mansell's *Vegetarianism and Manual Labour*, 10 April 1888 (Vegetarian Society, Manchester, 1897) [Bodleian Library, Oxford, Catalogue No. 16833 e14 (7)]. The pamphlet publications of the Manchester-based late Victorian and Edwardian Vegetarian Society reveal a remarkable body of ideas not only about health and diet, but also about social attitudes towards animals and the environment in general – ideas which we tend to take for granted today, yet which must have seemed very eccentric in 1890. Ernest Crosby and Elisée Ruclus' *The Meat Fetish: Two Essays on Vegetarianism* (Fifield, London, 1905) [Bodleian Library Catalogue No. 16833 e 14 (22)], speaks against blood sports and flogging, and in favour of 'Animal Rights'. I would recommend the bound volume of pamplets in the Bodleian Library [Cat. No. 16833 e14] to anyone interested in the history of vegetarianism.

3   Elisabeth Meyer-Renschhausen and Albert Wirz, 'Dietetics, Health Reform and Social Order: Vegetarianism as a Moral Physiology. The example of Maximilian Bircher-Benner', *Medical History* 43, 3 (July 1999), 323–41. The July 1999 number of *Medical History* is devoted to the definition and historical role of alternative and lay medicine, mainly in Holland and Germany.

4   Meyer-Renschhausen and Wirz [n.3], 327. Also Russell Sneddon, *About the Water Cure* (Thorson's Ltd., London, 1965), 7–10.

5   Roy Porter, *The Greatest Benefit to Mankind: A Medical History of Humanity from Antiquity to the Present* (Harper Collins, London, 1997), 396.

6   Maximilian Oskar Bircher-Benner, M.D., *Food Science for All. And a New Sunlight Theory of Nutrition. Lectures to Teachers of Domestic Economy* (trans. A. Eiloart (London, 1928)). Meyer-Renschhausen and Wirz [n.3], 334–40.

7   Robert Bell, M.D., *Reminiscences of an Old Physician* (Murray, London, 1924), 211–12. Bell does not appear in the 1930 *D.N.B.* Supplementary Volume, but is mentioned in *Who Was Who 1916–1928*, vol. II (London, 1947).

8   Robert Bell, *A Plea for the Treatment of Cancer without Operation* (London, 1919), 22–4. Bell, *Reminiscences* [n.7], 213.

9   Bell, *Reminiscences* [n.7], 271–4.

10   Robert Bell, *Dietetics and Hygienics versus Disease* (Psycho-Therapeutic Society, London, 1910), 22: Bell claimed that when he qualified in 1868, only 5–6 pounds of meat purchased per head of population was imported into Britain, but by 1910 it had grown to 50 pounds. This was, of course, in addition to home-produced supplies. One suspects, however, that the meat consumed per head of the British population might not have risen quite so dramatically during this period, for the introduction of refrigeration in the 1870s and the opening up of the market for frozen meat from Australasia and America did great damage to English agriculture over the same period, as reflected in the late Victorian slump in agricultural land values.

11   *Health for All*, June 1927. As early as 1902, however, 'The Vegetarian Society Health Food Store, 19, Oxford Street, Manchester' was offering a wide range of butter and lard substitutes, along with basic vegetarian cooking ingredients, as well as biscuits and jams. These late Victorian vegetarians were not starvation devotees, and seemed to enjoy a hearty meat-free diet. Advertisement in F.D. Newell, *Colds: Their Cause and Natural Cure, with Hints for the Maintenance of Health and Prevention and Cure of Diseases in General* (Broadbent, Manchester, 1902) [Bodleian Library Catalogue No. 16833 e14 [14]].

12 *Health for All*, March 1928, back cover, advertises 'Champneys', 'The World Famous Home of Health', 'Where *Healing* is the Natural Thing'. On 2 August 1999 I spoke to two gentlemen with a long acquaintance with Tring, one of whom was a retired physician. They spoke with warm approval of the local baker's shop which had supplied 'Champneys' with wholemeal bread products in the days when such things were not readily available. The smells, and the bread itself, were superb!

13 F. Yeats-Brown, 'The Fasting Cure', *Health for All*, June 1927, 9–10.

14 Revd Walter Wynn, *How I cured Myself by Fasting, Being the Marvellous Story of a Fifty-Two-Days' Fast* (Rider & Co., London, undated; Bodleian Library statutory acquisition stamp 10 February 1927), 9–25.

15 Wynn, *How I Cured Myself* [n.14], 29, 34.

16 Wynn, *Fasting, Exercise, Food and Health for Everybody* (Rider & Co., London, undated, *c.*1929), 34.

17 C.M. Trelawny Irving, 'Fasting for Fifty-two Days', *Health for All*, June 1927, 20.

18 Upton Sinclair's 'Perfect Health', *Contemporary Review* 532 (London, April 1910), 428–40, and published simultaneously in *Cosmopolitan*, New York, 1910, caused quite a sensation amongst those 'seeking their health' on both sides of the Atlantic in 1910. Its very title 'Perfect Health' suggests the finding of that very key to wholeness for which all the 'unwell' searched. Sinclair followed it up with another article five months later, where he claimed that 'No magazine article that I have ever written has attracted so much attention as "Perfect Health"': this was Sinclair's 'On Fasting', *Contemporary Review* 537 (Sept. 1910), 380–4. In this second article Sinclair published some of the correspondence which he had received in response to 'Perfect Health', which is in itself not only an eye-opener into the world of American health-seekers in 1910, but discusses the 'Milk Diet', and the recent fad of 'Fletcherism', which seems to have been based on prolonged food-chewing.

19 This was, no doubt, the 'Lecture at Finsbury Park by Dr Stanley J. Lief, the Principal of the nature cure home at Tring', reported in *Health for All*, June 1927, 27. The printed account gives a valuable insight into Lief's medical thinking. Lief did not believe that germs caused disease, but that they 'were only a result of diseased conditions and were not a cause' – a commonly-held belief in the naturopathic movement. His title 'Doctor' was not recognised by the medical profession.

20 Bernarr MacFadden, *Fasting for Health. A Complete Guide to How, When, and Why to use the Fasting Cure* (MacFadden Publications Inc., New York, 1923), viii.

21 S.J. Lief, 'Champney's Chat. News from the Home of Health', *Health for All*, June 1927, 16.

22 Stella Lief, D.P., N.D., 'Making motherhood easy', *Health for All*, April 1928, 376–8. (Various configurations of qualification letters are added to the names of Diet Reform writers, and I am not exactly certain what they mean: 'N.D.' could be 'Naturopathic Doctor'. By 1920, moreover, there were various institutions in America from which one could obtain such qualifications, though they were not recognised by the orthodox medical profession.)

23 Philip Milwood, 'Natural Living and the Child', *Health for All*, April 1928, 367.

24 Margaret Brady, M.Sc., *Children's Health and Happiness* (Health for All Pub. Co., London, 1948), 35–6.

25 Bernarr MacFadden, *Building of Vital Power. Deep Breathing and a Complete System for Strengthening the Heart, Lungs, Stomach and all the Great Vital Organs* (Physical Culture Publishing Co., New York, 1904). *Vital Power* seems to have been about the unleashing of some special force within the individual. Some of his other titles conveyed the 'body beautiful' message: *Superb Virility of Manhood*, and, with Marion Malcolm, *Health–Beauty–Sexuality. From Girlhood to Womanhood* (both Physical Culture Publishing Co.), advertised on the end papers of *Building of Vital Power*; however, I have not been able to locate copies.

26 Lief, 'Lecture at Finsbury Park' [n.19], 22. Perhaps Lief picked up the word from the writings of Dr Robert Bell, who in his *Reminiscences* [n.7], 272, used the phrase 'auto toxaemia' for poisons ingested from a sluggish colon.

27 George R. Clements, LL.B., N.D., 'How to cure Chronic Catarrh', *Health for All*, April 1928, 366, 368.

28 Clements, 'Catarrh' [n.27], 368.

29 George R. Clements, *The Villainy of Vaccination* (Health for All Pub. Co., undated, Bodleian Library statutory acquisition stamp 27 October 1927). This 45-page booklet, costing one shilling, was given a glowing announcement in *Health for All*, November 1927, 213.

30 This was no doubt the same Dr E. Frazer who wrote 'Are Germs the Cause or Effect of Disease?', *Health for All*, June 1929, 26–30. Like Clements, Lief, and others, he argues that illness is invariably a result of bad dietary habits, and that germs are a mere by-product of the process.

31 Clements, *Vaccination* [n.29], 13–14.

32 Clements, *Vaccination* [n.29], 35.

33 Benedict Lust, N.D., D.O., M.D., 'Cancer: its causes and cure', *Health for All*, June 1927, 17.

34 'Harry Clements, N.D., D.O. (Member of the Nature Cure Association), 60 Warwick Gardens, Kensington. 9 a.m.–6 p.m.' Advertisement, *Health for All*, October 1928, 192.

35 Harry Clements, N.D., D.O., *Appendicitis, its Prevention and Treatment by Natural Methods* (Lutterworth, London, undated; Bodleian Library statutory acquisition stamp 28 November 1928).

36 Harry Clements, D.O., *Banishing Backache and Disc Trouble* (Health for All Pub. Co., London, 1952), 23. In Clements' *Diets to Help Prostate Troubles* (Thorson's, Wellingborough, 1978), 27–8, he recommended a 'Semi-Fast' with water and fresh fruit juices to treat prostate problems.

37 Rather curiously, Dr Robert Bell had argued that human beings were designed to be vegetarians, as 'neither man's

teeth nor his digestive organs were ever intended to deal with the flesh of animals', Bell, *Reminiscences* [n.7], 233.

38 G. Melvyn Howe, *Man, Environment and Disease in Britain. A Medical Geography through the Ages* (Pelican, 1972), 176 for 1840, and Table 9, p.212, for 1920s.

39 George Orwell, *The Road to Wigan Pier* (London, 1937), Chapter VI (p.88 in Penguin edn. 1989).

40 Wynn, Fasting [n.16], 34.

41 Mansell, *Vegetarianism and Manual Labour* [n.2]. A four-page pamphlet, selling for one halfpenny.

42 S. Fulder, *The Handbook of Complementary Medicine* (Coronet Books, Hodder and Stoughton, London, 1984), cited in Douglas Black, 'Complementary (Alternative) Medicine', in *The Oxford Medical Companion*, ed. John Walton, Jeremiah A. Barondess and Stephen Lock (O.U.P., 1994), 159–61.

7   A tenacious survival: the classical tradition today

1 Related by Dr B. practising in Salford: private communication, June 1981.

2 Related to me in conversation following a lecture I delivered to the Abernethian Society, at St Bartholomew's Hospital, London, in February 1982. Many medical friends have repeated to me how, for the sake of simplicity, they will use 'blood-thinning' explanations to patients with cardiovascular complaints. It is also surprising how many otherwise well-educated patients assume that their blood thickens with age. I recall a conversation with an elderly gentleman in Manchester who had spent most of his life in accountancy, telling me in good faith that his doctor had prescribed some 'blood-thinning' tablets to cure his heart problem.

3 The intermixing of English, Irish and Welsh words when describing disease symptoms was made apparent in the discussion which developed following a lecture which I delivered to the Liverpool Medical Institution in May 1986. I wish to thank Mr Eric Strach, F.R.C.S. and others

for supplying me with information, and pointing me towards further fruitful lines of enquiry.

4   Culpeper the Herbalist is one of several such firms. A similar enterprise is that of Crabtree and Evelyn, though they tend more to specialise in 'natural' cosmetics and toiletries. The highly successful 'Body Shop' chain also tends to retail herbal toiletries rather than medicinal substances. There are, however, several shops which clearly specialise in therapeutic preparations, including one with which I am familiar in Oxford, opened in 1987, which sells herbs by weight in a reproduction Victorian interior.

5   Stanley J. Lief, 'The Editor's Stand-point.....' 'The Doctor of To-morrow', *Health for All*, April 1928, 364.

6   Dr Trevor Smith's *The Principles, Art and Practice of Homeopathy,* Insight Editions (Worthing, 1985) provides a good account of modern homeopathic medicine. It is very interesting to see how it draws on the ancient traditions, and is almost reminiscent of John Weslsey in its castigation of the 'synthetic mechanistic approach of computerised medicine,' p.16. It classifies human types in accordance with homeopathic affinities, and puts great stress on balance. Richard Grossman's *The Other Medicines*, Pan Original (1986), gives a good account of current alternative medical ideas, including the diagnosis of disease by the visual examination of the sufferer's foot, 263–265.

7   These posters were displayed in Manchester Piccadilly Station (amongst other places) in the autumn of 1987.

8   The appalling backwardness – medical and otherwise – of the Appalachian region of Eastern Tennessee in 1917 is recorded by Dr May Cravath Wharton in her *Doctor Woman of the Cumberlands* (Uplands, Pleasant Hill, Tennessee, 1953). See also William E. Fowler, 'Folk Remedies and Belief in Maury County, 1936' in *Tennessee Folklore Society Bullein*, Vol. LIII, I, Middle Tennessee State University, Murfreesboro, Tennessee, Spring 1988, 7–26. I am also indebted to Dr Eleanor Drake-Mitchell, of Cookville, Tennessee, for this response.

9   In September 1986 I delivered the 'Grand Rounds' lecture, on the subject of the survival of classical language in modern folk-medicine, to the Department of Surgery, University of Minnesota. The discussion which followed resulted in several new examples being pointed out to me by medical persons in the audience. The examples related crossed European, American Indian and Latin American traditions, all of which relied upon humorally-associated ideas. In January 1987 I delivered a similar lecture to the Fargo Clinic and Medical Association, Fargo, North Dakota, which resulted in further examples being brought to my attention.

10   It must be remembered that Greek medical ideas not only passed into northern Europe, but also into medieval Islam, by which route they travelled to Arabia and India. In 1500, academic physicians in Stockholm, Paris, Baghdad and Calcutta would have shared a remarkably similar academic medical culture, thereby explaining the transmission of these ideas over a large part of the Earth's surface. An excellent account of Asian medical practice in the contemporary West is Mohammed Aslam's 'The practice of Asian medicine in the United Kingdom', Nottingham University Ph.D. thesis, Department of Pharmacy (1979): see pp.33–34 and more for an account of the stress placed upon humoral balance and the properties of heat and cold in Hakim medicine. Dr Aslam's Chapter 1 reviews the strands of Asian medicine currently practised in the West, including homeopathy and herbalism. I am indebted to Marlene Hinshelwood, of the Race Relations Commission, for drawing my attention to this reference. See also Hakim Mohammed Said's 'Potential of Herbal Medicines in Modern Medical Therapy,' a paper published by The Second International Conference on Islamic Medicine, Kuwait, 29 March–2 April 1982.

11   Don Frame, 'Law Traps "Cure for Cancer" Salesman', *Manchester Evening News,* 17 January 1998, front page. The salesman was given a three-year conditional discharge with £590 costs, under the Cancer Act of 1939.

Index

Index

Index

Index

Wild West shows, 113
Willis, Thomas, 26, 170
Winkfield, Alfred, 164
Wirz, Albert, 191, 192
womb, 50, 61
Woodward, John, 173, 186
workhouses, 93, 95
World War I, 7, 84, 93, 95, 100, 111, 165, 183
World War II, 49, 98, 104, 147, 187
Worsley, 175, 183
Wroe, Bob, 103

Wynn, Walter, 135, 136, 144, 193, 196

X-rays, 27

Yeats-Brown, F., 134, 193

Zola, Emile, 4, 163